THE
$1,000,000
DESKTOP
PUBLISHING
IDEA BOOK

by Richard Nodine

Library of Congress Catalog Card Number 94-66129

ISBN 0-9641100-0-8
Pacific Learning Council
251 Post Street, Suite 300
San Francisco, CA 94108

NOTICE

The contents of this book reflect the author's views acquired through experience in the field under discussion. The author is not engaged in rendering any legal professional service. The services of a professional are recommended if legal advise or assistance is needed. The publisher and/or author disclaim any personal loss or liability caused by utilization of any information presented herein. The author and publisher cannot and will not guarantee your satisfaction in any dealing with sources mentioned in this book.

INTRODUCTION

In the early 1980's Apple Computer Corporation sold the first desktop laser printer and Aldus introduced PageMaker. The awesome power of these two technical advances is yet to be realized. Ten years later, the vast majority of desktop publishing systems are used for nothing more than enhanced typing stations. A few visionaries have pushed the limits of computer-based publishing, but their work has been largely technical in nature. Our objective is to reveal the virtually limitless possibilities of this burgeoning industry and suggest ways that average people can become participants in the global information explosion for less than the cost of an average used car.

Will everyone who reads this book make a million dollars? Of course, there is no way to know, although its perfectly conceivable than many people will. We have intentionally provided a wide range of ideas for the application of desktop publishing systems. The reader may choose to work their way from the more modest to the most ambitious or simply generate a comfortable part-time in come for themselves. Diversity of application is one of the exciting aspects of "desktop." The title of the book really has more to do with the value of the concepts it contains. If this seems a bit conceited, we apologize. But, we had to get your attention and our motive is well founded in the marketing strategies we will discuss later. For better or worse, the most effective way to quickly establish value in our culture is through a reference to money. We sincerely hope you will feel our title is justified and that you profit from this book in relation to your expectations.

Some bemoan the fact that this technology has proliferated mediocre writing and design in the thinly veneered wrap of typography. To some degree this is true. We prefer to see the other side of the coin; an end to the capricious and arbitrary domination of the publishing establishment that once played gatekeeper to the world's knowledge. Who knows how many James Joyces or Saul Bellows received rejection notices from assistant editors who lacked the vision to appreciate their work. This will soon be a thing of the past. With the proliferation of personal computers and their ability to transmit words, sounds and images over a gigantic fiber-optic network we will all become publishers, able to disseminate our most intimate thoughts to every corner of the globe. But, that's another book. Today we are exploring just a few of the empowering possibilities that rather basic electronic prepress systems have created for every literate member of society who has a desire to express themselves in print.

This book will always be a work in progress. For that reason we published two editions, one perfect bound and one comb-bound. The perfect bound edition is less current, and therefore less expensive, the comb bound edition is duplicated on a Xerox machine and shipped the same day orders are received. In this way we are able to provide the very latest data to our customers. This is important in three areas:

1. Technical advances - Because we make equipment recommendations a three year old copy of this book may be misleading. In fact, the hardware and software industries are moving so rapidly that several changes had to be made while the book was being written.

2. Resource information - Although we try to present the most current data on established companies we are frequently surprised that suppliers have consolidated, moved or gone out of business entirely. Conversely, new resources are constantly coming to our attention.

3. Desktop Applications - Almost everyday someone finds a new way to exploit this marvelous technology. We want to expose our readers to the widest range of possibilities. Therefore, we invite you to share your brain-

storms with us (and our readers.) Although we will credit you with your idea (if you like) we are unable to pay for submissions. Why then should you share your idea so broadly? Isn't it good business to keep ideas secret from your competition? We think not! Ideas fill the cosmos, they swirl around us everywhere. They have the ability to stimulate thought and bring like-minded people together. But they have no monetary value until they are coupled with actions and the investment of time and resources. Unlike a secret bank account, a pool of ideas can be opened to the world, thus enriching everyone without diminishing the value of the originator. In fact, the originator is enriched too, by the recognition and personal contacts he gains from his efforts. Send us your best ideas. We'll see they are put to good use.

CONTENTS

WHAT IS DESKTOP PUBLISHING

Although the term "desktop publishing" became popular in the early 1980's it is already outmoded. After all where else would you publish, on the floor? The terms was originally a reaction to the amazement many people felt when they discovered that much of the traditional cameras, typesetters, and stripping departments normally associated with the creation of printed material could be replaced with a microcomputer, scanner and laser printer that could literally be housed on a desktop.

This has never been entirely true. Even at this writing, the production of a sophisticated full color document still requires a larger computer than you would normally place on a desktop. Most professional color reproduction can be "specified" by microcomputers but the actual assembly must still be done in the traditional manner or by large computer based systems like those produced by Heil or Scitex. These systems are designed and dedicated to the production of color printing plates and have the huge memory capacity required to store and manipulate color images. Desktop or microcomputer based publishing is still limited to one color, spot color and presentation color documents.

The advent of the laser printer made the production of handsome one color documents affordable to practically every business and individual. The laser printer interprets data from a word processing program (like Microsoft Word) or a page layout program (like PageMaker) and produces the typeset page by use of heat sensitive toner deposited on the paper, very much like a Xerox machine. One color documents are usually printed in black and white. The document may be produced in small quantities directly from a laser printer or the laser printer original may be used as a master to reproduce larger quantities via Xerography or offset printing.

PRESENTATION GRAPHICS

Cannon LaserColor®
Copier

An exciting new field created by desktop technology is color presentation graphics. The lavish use of color used to be cost effective only on long press runs. Today desktop designers can create full color brochures, posters, charts, even entire books in quantities of one or two. The Cannon LaserColor® Copier with a computer interface takes most of the credit for this breakthrough. This copier is also a color scanner with a capacity of 400 d.p.i. (dots per inch). A skillful operator can scan-in color photography through the LaserColor® Copier, place it in a drawing or page layout program, add text, charts and headlines, and output a beautiful full color document in about two of hours.

Because the Cannon LaserColor® Copier and its necessary support devices costs about $120,000.00 it is usually purchased by large corporations and service bureaus. The service bureau is a business that invests in desktop technology and makes it available to individuals and small businesses on a time-rental or per-piece basis. There are service bureaus in most metropolitan centers offering Cannon LaserColor® service along with Linotronic high resolution printers. Most of these service bureaus also offer computers for rent by the hour.

35mm slides

Many service bureaus also offer 35mm slide generation from images composed in various drawing and presentation programs such as Aldus Persuasion. This can be yet another source of income for the desktop publisher. As competition grows, sales professionals and executives need increasingly sophisticated tools to make dramatic presentations. There are several good programs available for the generation of slides and overhead transparencies. Ask your local service bureau which programs they support.

Another computer based presentation technique, still in its infancy *plotter graphics* is the color plotter graphic poster. The plotter was originally developed to reproduce architect's and engineer's drawings from computer data but it has been adapted to generate large scale drawing, graphs and posters from several popular drawing programs. The plotter can output a graphic 40" to 50" wide by almost any length. Larger art can be tiled (printed in sections). If your local service bureau doesn't offer this service you can find it via mail order in the back of popular computer magazines.

WHY PUBLISH

Its a well established fact, we are far more likely to believe information received from the printed page than in any other form. How many times have you heard some one say, 'I saw it in the paper so it must be true?' Naturally, this is an over simplification, but it does express our unconscious tendency to believe what we read more readily than what we hear. Most people studied report a tendency to assign greater credibility to newspapers and other print media journalism than to broadcast media.

Prior to a sales meeting many organizations go to great expense to *the power of print* prepare elaborate brochures for their representatives. Although the prospect knows there may be only a dozen copies of the brochure in existence, the dramatic power of the printed word is often a deciding factor in a successful presentation.

Whenever you need to convince someone to do something, be sure to enlist the aid of print. Statistics are especially impressive when presented in print. A written testimonial carries far greater weight than the statement, "Harry thought it was a good idea."

Prior to the advent of electronic publishing many printing techniques developed including letterpress, gravure, screen printing, flexography and lithography. We will concentrate on the most popular and economical printing form available today, offset lithography. This technique is employed in many forms to produce everything from the simplest handbill to elaborate full-color books. Some examples include:

types of printing

1. SINGLE COLOR LINE ART is the most basic form of printing. It consists of black or colored type on white or colored stock. It may also include graphic devices such as lines or bars that embellish the page. It can even include drawings or illustrations as long as they are pure black and white. Many artists will create drawings that employ a cross-hatch or a stipple pattern to give an illusion of gray tones. These drawings can still be reproduced as line art because no photo-mechanical techniques are required to render the drawings.

2. MULTICOLORED LINE ART is very similar to single color line art except that it uses multiple colors. These colors are applied to separate elements on the page. For instance, the type may be black and the rule lines that surround the page may be blue. Headlines and body copy (the largest mass of text on a page) may be different colors. Illustrations or dingbats (printers term for small symbol, usually at the end of a block of copy, having no particular meaning) may be set off in yet another color. On small presses the sheets must be run through the press once for each color. Larger presses can run up to eight colors in one "pass". Colors may be specified from a printer's own chart or from the Pantone Matching System (see process color).

Spot color documents are almost always offset printed from color separations generated on the laser printer or a high resolution printer like the Linotronic 300. The Linotronic Printer and other high resolution printers can reproduce the data from a word processing program or page layout program with much greater accuracy than a laser printer. They use a photographic method to create an image, therefore the pages must be "developed" after they come out of the printer. The increased accuracy and resolution of these machines comes at substantially greater cost. Although most service bureaus charge about 30 cents a page for laser prints, they charge about $10.00 per page for Linotronic output.

Linotronic printers

Most page layout and drawing programs will produce either composite proofs (everything you see on the screen is rendered in shades of gray) or color separations. When the color separation option is chosen each color is represented by solid black on a separate sheet of paper or film. Small register marks automatically generated by the program on the outside edges of the sheet tell the printer how to assemble the color to achieve the desired results.

When a document's colors are separated by areas of blank paper the document is said to have *loose registration*. Loosely registered documents can be successfully printed from laser printed masters at 300 to 400 dot per inch (dpi) resolution. Documents in which the colors touch or overlap to form additional colors are said to have *tight registration*. These documents should be printed from high resolution masters at 1250 to 2500 dpi. When you supply your offset printer with paper positives he may make *direct paper plates*. These are suitable for one color or very loose two color printing. More complex jobs require metal plates that are created from film negatives. If you supply your printer with film negatives direct from a high-resolution source like the Linotronic 300 you will get the best possible results. This will allow the offset printer to burn his printing plate directly from your original film with no interim steps needed.

tight and loose registration

metal vs paper plates

3. HALFTONE is a photomechanical process that converts the gray tones in an artists illustration or photograph into tiny black dots, thus allowing the press to render what appears to be a continuous scale of grays. Look at black and white photos from your newspaper under a magnifying glass. You'll see the intricate pattern of dots that form the gray tones. The original photo or illustration is actually photographed

halftones

through a screen of dots to create this effect. The process is also called *screening* a photo. The technique can also be used without a photo to create areas of additional color on a page. For instance, if you are already printing red and would also like to print pink, you might add an area of red *screened back to 50%* This means that instead of printing red at 100% you would add a fine dot pattern reducing the red to 50% of its intensity. Because your eye mixes the red dots with the white of the paper you will achieve the effect of pink. Naturally, if you printed 80% red the pink would appear darker. If you printed 20% red the pink would appear lighter.

holding a screen   Different press are capable of **holding** different patterns. The 65 line screen that most newspapers and instant printers use is relatively course. It means that each linear inch of photo contains 65 rows of dots. Many magazines and books use 133 line screens. These render far better detail. Very fine printers may use 200 line screens or higher. Always check with your printer to determine what line screens they are capable of holding on their press.

four color process   **4. PROCESS COLOR** is the technique through which full color images are photomechanically reduced to cyan (blue), yellow, magenta (a bluish red), and black and then printed on a four color press. The color separations are made by an engraver using elaborate photographic filters, or by computers. The engraver must assemble the four layers of film produced in the color separation process with other film representing the type and line elements of the page. This process is called stripping and it is sometimes done by the printer. Modern computers have eliminated much of this tedious work by allowing the operator to compose entire pages on the computer screen and print them out in continuous sheets.

process color tints   The designer may also use colors on the page that do not exist in the photo or illustration. If these colors are produced by combining the four process colors they are called **tints**. In especially high quality printing the designer may wish to use solid colors not made by combining process colors. This gives the designer more flexibility and makes the colors stronger and more pure. These colors are usually called PMS colors after the Pantone Matching System, a patented color system that has universal acceptance among printers. Pantone or PMS colors are specified by numbers and Pantone books are available in many forms from commercial art supply stores.

Pantone® Colors

Each form of printing can exist on a page by itself or in combination with any or other form.

WHY DESKTOP?

Why is desktop publishing superior to conventional typing:

proportional spacing

1. Desktop publishing uses typesetting techniques. Unlike a typewriter, typesetting employs ***proportional letter-spacing*** resulting in a more densely packed page. The desktop publisher uses fewer sheets of paper than the typist to display the same number of words. This can result in substantial savings in a long document copied many times.

multiple columns

2. The desktop publisher can manipulate text more easily than the typist. Documents can have multiple columns, a variety of type faces, and bold or italicized type. Properly used, these features add to the readability of a document.

integrated graphics

3. The desktop publisher can integrate photos, drawings and charts directly with the text. This saves readers the time and inconvenience usually associated with referencing those items on separate pages.

4. Well composed pages from experienced desktop publishing designers are more aesthetically pleasing, dramatic and therefore are more likely to be read than those produced through conventional typing techniques.

Remember, cheep documents are not usually cost effective because they are seldom read, and even more seldom taken seriously.

DESKTOP & DESIGN

The graphic design industry has been radically altered in the last ten years. Virtually every designer with a serious practice has been forced to purchase or access a computer system to remain competitive. Prior to desktop publishing, the graphic designer would indicate their layout or design on paper, specify the type position and have an outside type service set the type. This was very expensive and resulted in long delays when revisions were required. Today the designer works on the screen with the exact type that will appear on the finished page. Revisions are made quickly and efficiently and the client receives an excellent proof of the job before costly hours are committed to composite films. Most graphic designers have embraced the new technology with great enthusiasm.

However, many desktop publishers are entering the field from other disciplines, namely computer technology and clerical backgrounds. We frequently hear publishers say, "We aren't really designers, we just know what we think looks good." Well, that's what a designer is, someone who knows how to make something look good. In fact, a good typist is really a graphic designer. Modern typewriters allow far more flexibility than printing presses of only a few years ago.

The truth is, anyone who causes marks to be made on a page is a graphic designer. The good ones take responsibility for their design. They look at the pages they produce and criticize them for balance, tension, contrast and legibility. They use each job as an opportunity to explore new techniques, formats and layouts, thus enhancing their skill and broadening their repertoiré. The poor designers say, "I'm just a technician, not a designer." And they use this rational to continue to produce second-rate documents.

WHAT MAKES A GOOD PAGE?

Many attempts have been made to distill the design process to a list of do's and don'ts. Most of these attempts fail because they ignore the essential question behind the production of every document:

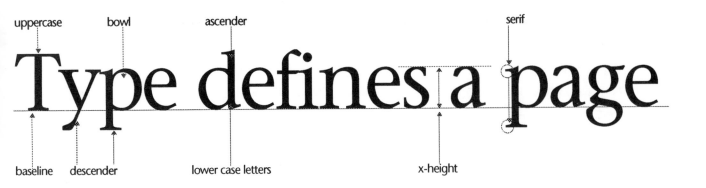

uppercase   bowl   ascender   serif

baseline   descender   lower case letters   x-height

STONE SERIF
Type defines a page

FUTURA BOOK
Type defines a page

STONE SERIF BOLD
Type defines a page

FUTURA BOLD
Type defines a page

STONE SERIF BOLD ITALIC
Type defines a page

FUTURA BOLD ITALIC
Type defines a page

STONE SERIF ITALIC
Type defines a page

FUTURA BOOK ITALIC
Type defines a page

STONE SERIF SEMIBOLD
Type defines a page

FUTURA LIGHT
Type defines a page

STONE SERIF SEMIBOLD ITALIC
Type defines a page

FUTURA LIGHT ITALIC
Type defines a page

FUTURA SEMIBOLD
Type defines a page

84 POINTS   72 POINTS   48 POINTS   36 POINTS   24   18   14   12   10   9   8   6

10

How do you want your reader to respond to your document?

You must first answer this question before you can design your page.

Do you want to create the impression that you represent an aggressive, dynamic organization such as a sales or marketing firm? Do you want to give the impression of quiet, detached professionalism appropriate to a bank, doctor or attorney? What is the over-all tone of your document? Whether you are creating documents for your own company or for hire, its a good idea to collect examples from other organizations in the same industry. Examine them for type style, spacing, the use of bold or large headlines, graphic devices such as star bursts and other elements to add emphasis or attract attention.

determine design objectives

Exactly how do you want your reader to digest your document. If you publish a general interest newsletter to a large organization you may want to use large bold headlines to identify the beginning of each article. In this way, your reader is free to pick the articles that interest him. You may also want to add a front page "highlights column" that lists the important features of your paper and their location in the paper.

On the other hand publishers of single topic reports may decide to use smaller "inter-headlines" (small topic heads that identify sections of an article) to break long boring columns of type and help readers who want to skim the report for key features. Publishers of fiction or highly technical papers who want to discourage skimming will use "pull quotes" (enlarged phrases or sentences pulled from the text, often used in lieu of illustrations) to enliven their pages without assisting the casual reader to skip important data. At the far extreme, the publisher of an important medical or legal document may decide that all their data is so vital that it must be read word for word. This publisher may decide to forgo all graphic conventions for straight columns of type. Few people will read such a dry paper, but those who do will probably read it the way it was intended.

establish order of importance

Create a hierarchy of importance in your document. What do you want your reader to see first, second, third, etc.? Give these elements progressively less weight in relation to their importance. Remember, if something is more important, other things must be less important. The novice publisher will often create pages containing 10 elements screaming for attention with equal volume. This only achieves reader annoyance.

the grid

The basis of good page design is a strong underlying grid. The gird may be partially visible in the form of rule lines or column breaks, or it may be visible only to the designer. But, in either case it holds the elements of the page in place in a logical, and visually pleasing way. It also lends continuity to multiple page documents. One of the most important skills of a desktop designer is the ability to construct a grid that is flexible enough to allow reasonable variety within the document yet rigid enough to provide the continuity a reader needs. All good page layout programs allow great flexibility in the construction of the document grid. Consult your specific software manuals for more instructions, but never start a page without considering the construction of the underlying grid.

UNDERSTANDING TYPE

Type is the basis of all language. It is the series of symbols we use to convey meaning, not only in a literal sense, through the combination of letters to create words, but through the choice of type faces we use to imply a context for our words. Today's print buyer can choose from thousands of type faces that add meaning to their messages. The key to good typography is in selecting a type face that evokes the same image your words convey. Type also gives the page color and texture. Different faces have different textures. Developing a sensitivity to the color and texture of your type allows you to compose more interesting pages.

The greatest double edge blessing/curse of desktop publishing is the vast selection of typefaces available to the publisher.

Inexperienced desktop technicians, especially those with a computer or clerical background, are inclined to use every typeface they own on their first page. The results are hideous! More experienced designers are always more conservative in their selection of faces.

use type conservatively

All typefaces are divided by form into two general categories; *serif faces* that are drawn with tabs at the end of each stroke, and *san serif faces* that lack these tabs. Typefaces are then subcategorized by families which often bare the name of the designer who created them. For instance, Caslon was created by the English designer William Caslon *(1692 - 1766)*. It was used to print the original publication of the Declaration of Independence and it remains popular today. Like many classic typefaces, it has been modified over the years by many designers and type foundries. But each modification has been intended to adapt the face to new technology while preserving the basic beauty and grace of the original design. There are several fonts within the Caslon family including; Caslon, Caslon Bold, Caslon Italic, Caslon Bold Italic, Caslon Swash (an ornate initial capitol used to begin a document or important section). Other type families contain even more variety. Some, like the contemporary Stone family include both serif and sanserif faces.

serif vs san serif type

Type is also divided into two functional categories; *headline type* and *body type*. The same type face may be used in both headlines and body (the main text of a page) or your may choose different type faces for both.

headline vs text type

Type is measured in points. There are 72 points to an inch. However, a 72 point letter is not one inch high. The 72 points include the space occupied by the upper case (capital) letter plus the descenders of the lower case letters.

type measurement

We call the space between lines of type *leading* after the lead bars used in antique movable type presses. If type is used without leading we say it is *set solid.* Setting type solid allows you to get more words

leading

copy fitting   on a page but the words will be more difficult to read and less attractive than type set with a few points of leading. When we specify type and leading we do it as a fraction with the type size on top and the total height of the type and leading on the bottom. For instance, 10/14 indicates 10 point type with 4 points of leading. This is an average text specification. Various type faces look better with varying amounts of leading. Experience will train your eye to use each type face to its best advantage. By changing the amount of leading and the point size of the type we may also change the color and texture of the page.

the design of type   The process of designing typefaces is a complex and demanding task. Over the centuries our eyes have become accustom to highly refined characters, drawn by masters of the art of typography and further refined by digital computers. For this reason, the novice is encouraged to employ one of the thousands of type faces available and leave innovation to professionals. Today we have basically three sources for type; the commercial type house, computer generated type, and transfer type. Of these three options, computer generation is the most convenient and cost effective for those who work with type on a regular basis.

PUBLISHING BC (BEFORE COMPUTERS)

Life in the publishing biz was not always a bed of roses. In fact, there are still many survivors from the pre-electronic age practicing today. If only to provide a more thorough understanding of the wonders of modern computers, we feel obligated to give the reader a brief over-view of the processes of print preparation prior to circa 1985. You may even find isolated projects in which these archaic techniques are useful.

Let's assume we have prepared written text of the appropriate length. Therefore, the challenge is to put that text in some form that will produce an attractive, professional looking printed page. Because a special copy camera is used to transfer your images to the printing plate, this form is called *camera ready art* or *CRA*. It means your copy has been prepared in pure black and white (no shades of gray). CRA includes clear indications of the edges of the page. This can be done by simply positioning your copy on an 8.5" x 11" sheet of paper, exactly as you want it to appear on the final printed page, then giving it to your printer. This is a common practice in the instant-printing industry.

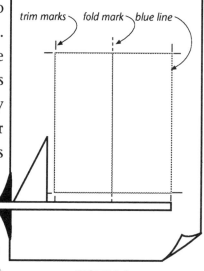

FIGURE A

A more precise method *(FIGURE A)* involves gluing the copy and all other visual elements to a board, larger than the actual printed page. Each element is placed in the position it

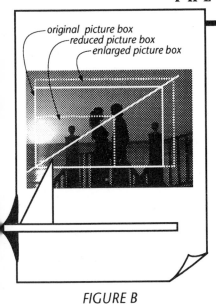

original picture box
reduced picture box
enlarged picture box

FIGURE B

will occupy on the final print. The edges of the page are indicated by lines drawn with a "non-repro blue" (light blue) pencil or pen, available from your art supply store. This pencil or pen produces a special color that the camera doesn't see when it transfers your copy to the printing plate. Tiny crop marks are made with a fine black pen outside the edge of the page. Solid crop marks indicate the trimmed edge of the page while broken or dotted crop marks indicate a fold line. This board is sometimes called a *paste-up* as it may consist of many items; drawings, charts and type, pasted to the board.

For truly professional results you should use a drawing board with a good parallel rule or t-square and a triangle to position copy and illustrations. Many art supply stores sell portable drawing boards that come already equipped with parallel rules. They also have light weight card stock preprinted with non-repro blue format grids. These are especially handy in positioning copy and illustrations because most of the tedious measuring is done for you. You simply align your copy to the grid. You can even see the grid through your paste-up by placing it on a light box or over a bright window. This helps you verify that all type is square to the blue grid lines. Use a wax stick to adhere the various elements to your paste-up. It will allow you to remove and reposition them later if necessary.

Velox prints   If you wish to include photographs, go to a local copy or photostat house and ask them to make a "screened paper positive" (sometimes called a Velox print) reduced to the actual size your paste-up requires. You could then position the print on your paste-up. If you wish to ad charts or other designs that will print in only black and white (no shades of gray), ask your copy shop to make PMTs (photo-mechanical transfers) of your designs at the correct scale. Trim these prints and add them to your paste-up. This technique is most often used when you are planning to take your job to an instant printing shop.

When your printed page consists of many complex items it may be more convenient for you to create a mechanical with a "key line drawing." If you are working with a quality printer you need not supply every element in exactly the correct scale. Create your paste-up on a board with your type in position. Then draw non-repro blue boxes to locate the other elements of your page. Use a *proportion wheel* to precisely calculate the height and width of all these elements in the same ratio as the original.

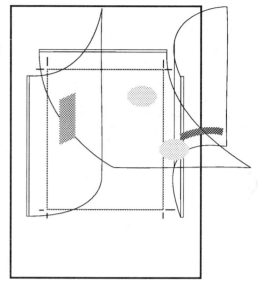

FIGURE C

For instance, suppose you have a black and white photograph 8" x 10". You may decide that your photo should be 3.5" wide to fit your page design. Your proportion wheel (available at most art and graphic supply stores) will tell you that you must reduce your photo to 37.5% and that the height will be approximately 3.75". Draw a box on your mechanical with a non-repro blue pencil to represent the photo at this final size. This is called a *key-line*.

The *box and diagonal* is another useful technique to proportion *scaling photos and art* photos and art. Make a tissue overlay for the photo and, using your triangle and t-square, draw a box around the part you wish to print. Draw a diagonal line through the box. You may now draw an enlarged or reduced box to fit your page design. Simply keep the sides of your new box square to the original box and be sure that the diagonal line intersects the two opposing corners of the new box *(FIGURE B)*. You'll want to code your key-line box and the photo so there will be no confusion about what element goes in which position.

Using the key-line technique produces better results because the printer will make the halftone on film and *strip* it directly into the film that is used to expose his printing plate. When you use a Velox print, (or PMT) the printer must rephotograph the entire page thus adding a *generation* of photography to the final image. Each time an photo or other element is rephotographed, xeroxed or reprinted we say it has gone through another generation. Each generation degrades the quality of the image. You have probably seen some brochures that were difficult to read because they had been re-copied so many times. Type begins to fall apart and photos gain contrast until they are pure black and white.

morie patterns   Another problem occurs when you reproduce photos from books and magazines. These photos have been screened already during their first printing process. A good printer can help you screen them satisfactorily but this is no job for an instant printer. Adding a second screen without special care causes an unsightly morie pattern to form across the image.

Creating a Multi-Color Line Art Mechanical

Follow the same steps to create the base mechanical. Place all the items on your base mechanical that will print black. Each additional color you add to your page requires an *overlay.* This is a sheet of transparent material like acetate, polyester or velum paper which is neatly taped to your base board outside the design area so that the overlay can be flipped back to reveal the base art. The overlay sheet should be larger than your page design but slightly smaller than the board on which you have placed your base art (black printer). If you are working with an instant printer you will make PMTs or screened positives of the elements you wish to print in the second color. Position them on the overlay, just as you positioned elements on the base layout. If you are working with a quality printer you may make keyline drawings on your overlays, just as you did on your base drawings.

using overlays to   You may add as many overlays as you need. Each overlay will in-
separate colors   dicate one color of your design. Your overlays may be taped outside all four margins of your base page so uncovering each layer is more convenient *(FIGURE C.)* It is necessary to use *register marks* on each overlay and the base board in case the layers of your mechanical are separated in the print preparation process. Register marks are small

designs composed of circles with cross hairs. You can purchase register marks as rub-down transfers or appliques. Place three register marks outside the margins of your base art, then place three more on each overlay so they precisely align to those on the base art.

typical register mark

Many designers use the single overlay technique when none of the colors on their page touch or come within one eighth inch of each other. Place all the images and type on the base art and tape a tissue overlay to the board. Circle each item and indicate its color on the overlay. If you are preparing a mechanical for a process color job you may indicate the location of your photos with key lines directly on your base art or on an overlay. You may assign process *tint* cclors to certain solid elements on your page. Remember, these are colors made of the four basic process colors. You many place these elements on the base art or on a separate overlay and indicate the tint you want in the margin. Refer to a special *tint selection book* available from your printer or art supply store .

Use the margins of your base art and overlays to make specific notations on how your want your page to appear. This is very important to the printer. They will interpret your instructions quite literally.

Special Effects

creating a reverse

Sometimes you will want white type to appear to come through a black or colored shape, like a black bar. This is called a *reverse* If you are working with an instant printer you must provide this reverse on your board. Have your copy shop make a *paper reverse* of the image and glue it to your paste-up. If you are working with a quality printer simply draw the solid shape on your base art or on the correct color overlay and provide the positive (black on white) type in position on a separate overlay.

The same technique works with photographs too. If you are using an instant printer you will need to have your copy or photostat shop create the *knock out.* This is a printers term for one image that appear

extra image needed for bleed

FIGURE D

to come through a photo. You then place the altered photo in your paste-up. If you are using a quality printer, you may simply provide the type you want knocked out in position on a separate overlay with instructions. In line or process color printing you may even choose to assign a color to your knocked out type.

You will want to include only part of a photograph in your printed page. You can alter the position of all four edges of the photo by *cropping*. The easiest way to visualize how your cropped photo will look is to cut two L shapes out of white paper or light weight board. Use them to form a picture frame over your photo and move them to view various segments of the photo until you have found a pleasing composition. In this way you may even change the height to width ratio of your photo.

visualizing cropped photos

Tape your paper Ls in position over your photo. If you are using an instant printer you will indicate the desired percent of enlargement or reduction of this cropped image and ask your stat house shoot a half-tone **Velox** (or PMT) to that size. If you are using a quality printer you may simply include a key line drawing at the correct percentage of enlargement or reduction on your mechanical.

creating silhouettes

If you want to use an isolated image from a photograph without showing its background you must create a **silhouette**. If the image you want to isolate is fairly complex (such as a person) your original photo should be no smaller than 8" x 10". Purchase sheets or rolls of Rubilith from your art supplier. This product is a mylar sheet with a thin transparent layer of red gelatine. Tape the Rubilith over your photograph and carefully trace the shape you wish to isolate with a #11 Exacto knife (also available from your art supplier). Peel off all the red gelatine from the sheet except where it covers the shape you want to print. Give the photo and overlay to your quality printer. He will do the rest. This technique is not possible with most instant printers, but it will work with both black and white quality printing and process color printing. Its important to remember that even if a photograph appears to have a white background the halftone process (or the color process) will assign a light gray dot pattern to it unless you use this silhouetting technique.

If you are preparing a complex mechanical its a good idea to include **position prints**. They tell to the printer just how you expect the finished job to look. These can be crude halftones photostats ordered from your stat house or Xerox copies made on a copier that has the ability to enlarge or reduce. They should be the exact size you want them to appear on the final page and cropped the same way. If you want the background dropped out you should remove the background on the position print. Glue your position prints to the base art or a separate overlay, if that is more convenient. In stead of position prints, many designers will trace the outstanding features of photos on an overlay and include it in position on the mechanical. Neither technique needs to be artfully executed but the printer does need a clear indication of what you expect on your page.

using position prints

An area of black or color that appears to run off the page in any direction is called a **bleed**. It may be a photograph that bleeds the page on four sides or a bar of color that runs off the right edge of the page, both are bleeds and are created in the same way. The image must be printed on a sheet larger than the final trimmed size you desire. The sheet is then trimmed down to finished size, thus removing part of the image. To prepare the mechanical you must allow $1/8$" of image to extend beyond the page trim marks indicated on your board. Some designers use sets of double trim marks to indicate this $1/8$" margin, thus ensuring there will be sufficient image to **bleed the trim** (FIGURE D).

creating bleeds

When printing a heavy a coverage of ink (much of the sheet is covered with ink) on coated paper you will probably want to print a varnish over your ink or the entire page. You may choose a *spot varnish*, just covering certain portions of the page, or a *flood varnish* that cov-

use of varnish

ers the entire page. Varnish is applied just like ink. If you want a spot varnish you need to prepare a mechanical to tell the printer just where it goes, as though it were another color ink. Varnishes may also be mat or gloss. You can use a *mat spot varnish* on a glossy paper (or vis a versa) to give certain areas of the page special emphasis. Many newer presses have the ability to apply electron beam or ultra-violet varnishes. These are plastic varnishes which do not dry but cure to a high water and wear resistant gloss, especially useful for book covers.

SPECIFYING TYPE

creating a layout Type may still be ordered to your specification from local type houses. Using a drawing board, parallel rule or t-square and triangle. Make a full scale sketch of how you want your printed page to appear. This is called your *layout*.

press type Use *press type*, available from most art supply stores, to compose your headlines. Most brands give specific instructions for use and proper application in their catalog. Your art supply dealer can also provide preprinted blueline format boards to make it easier to position the various elements of your layout. To estimate the length of your type columns you will need to employ the copy-fitting method.

copy fitting Copy fitting is the procedure used to measure the amount of space typewritten copy will occupy when set in type. It serves to determine the correct type size and line width needed to fit copy to a layout. The width of a column of type is measured in picas. A pica is 12 points. There are six picas to an inch. Every type face has a key number for each size in which it is available. This number is the average number of characters per pica x 10 or the average number of characters in a line 10 picas wide.

using key numbers To fit copy you must know; the number of characters in the typewritten copy (including spaces and punctuation), the key number of the type to be used (available from the type house catalog), and the area to be filled. If your copy was typed on an Elite model typewriter it will have 12 characters per liner inch. If it was typed on a Pica typewriter it will have 10 characters per inch.

Use a copy fitting wheel, available from your type house or commercial art supply store, to determine the characters per line you will achieve with any given type. Simply move the key number of the type you have chosen to the key arrow and read across the window until you find the width of your column in picas. To determine the vertical depth the type will occupy, use a Column Depth Scale, available with most copy fitting wheels. Be sure to add the depth of any leading to the height of the type when making this calculation and figure the depth of each paragraph separately.

copy fitting wheel

If your copy doesn't fill the space you want to occupy or over runs the space you may:
1. Adjust your leading,
2. Adjust your type size,
3. Adjust your column width and page margins,
4. Add or remove graphics that occupy space on the page.

WHAT DO YOU NEED?

If the preceding chapter seemed tedious it was because it described a process that was. Now are you ready to make a modest investment that will render the previous chapter obsolete?

HARDWARE

Because of the availability of service bureaus, desktop practitioners can operator in major cities with virtually no equipment investment. This is great for the entrepreneur with no capitol to bankroll their fledgling business, but it soon becomes evident that some equipment is helpful because:

1. Many jobs are emergencies that must be turned out at times when the service bureau is closed or equipment is otherwise occupied.
2. Using rental equipment is expensive. Far greater profits are possible with modest equipment investments.
3. Many clients will expect to see a well equipped office. You can't land many big accounts without the appearance of a professional operation.

The biggest mistake most publishers make is investing in second-rate, under-powered equipment. It becomes obsolete fast and the publisher ends up buying the better equipment and trading the original purchase for a salvage price (there is very little market for used computer equipment). Buy the best equipment you think you will ever need!

The debate over IBM (or IBM clone) vs Macintosh has raged for years and promises to continue until the end of time. The basic facts are:

1. You get more power per dollar in an IBM (or IBM clone) package *IBM vs Mac* than you do in a Macintosh package. (A clone is any PC that uses the same DOS operating system as does IBM, but is made by someone else.)

2. With the advent of Microsoft Windows, the IBM is easier to learn and operate (somewhat like a Macintosh). Many programs written for both IBM and Macintosh will run on both systems with special compatible drives.

3. As of this writing, most of the serious page layout and graphic programs are designed for the Macintosh platform.
4. Macintosh pricing has been reduced to make it somewhat more competitive with IBM.

If we were beginning a desktop business today we would conclude that our needs were best served by a Macintosh system, even at the higher cost. It will probably take years for IBM to achieve the prominence in graphics that Macintosh enjoys today. Shear power alone does not make a good publishing system. Moreover, the system of choice for most service bureaus you will use is Macintosh. Sure, most service bureaus have an old IBM over in the corner collecting dust, and they will fire it up occasionally if you talk nicely to them. But when you need fast dependable service you don't want to be treated as "the exception."

If you are adept at electronic finagling, you can create a very ac- *economy systems* ceptable, high powered Macintosh system with a cheep used Macintosh LC and some third party boards and a RasterOps two page monitor. The instructions for this and other Frankinstonian machinations can be found in popular computer magazines. However, if you aren't an engineer and you usually end up with many leftover parts from every childhood kit you assembled we strongly suggest you bite the bullet and purchase (or lease) equipment from a reputable dealer .

recommended package

We recommend a basic package consisting of:

1. A Macintosh Quadra 650 with 12 megabytes of RAM and 230 mega byte hard drive.
2. A SuperMac Spectrum/24 Series IV Accelerator
3. A SuperMac 20" Color Monitor
4. Apple Extended Keyboard & Mouse
5. A Varityper VT-400 Laserprinter with 11" x 17" paper capacity and 400 dot per inch output.
6. A UMAX 840M scanner with transparency adapter.

IMPORTANT UPDATE
As of this writing the consensus among professionals in our community is that a "wait and see" approach should be taken to the *Power PC*. It may prove to be a great time-saver, especially when using PhotoShop, but those of us who currently own working systems will probably wait at least a year before making the change-over. In this time we expect many of the yet unforeseen glitches in the new hardware, operating system and software to be resolved.

On the other hand, first time buyers may well wish to consider the Power PC. The added cost of working through the technical problems should be offset by the added speed.

With all reasonable cables (cables can be very expensive) this package can come to about $14,000.00. Actually it can be purchased for $13012.00 from PrePRESS DIRECT, 11 Mt. Pleasant Avenue, East Hanover, New Jersey 07936. This is an excellent value, well below list price for these items and the package includes Quark XPress at no additional cost (refer to their catalog volume 3.3).

pricing policies

Please understand, most computer equipment carries a *list price* and a *street price*. No one in their right mind pays the list price. That would be like to walking into a car showroom and offering to pay the sticker price for a car. Most urban centers have many reputable computer discounters who can be very helpful. Many will even come to your office and assist with the installation. The novice may want to purchase at least their basic system from such a dealer. Someone more experienced with computer purchasing and set-up (its really not all that difficult) will find additional savings through one of the many mail-order houses that advertise in MacWorld or MacUser magazine.

mail order buying

These mail-order operators offer a wider selection and better prices than many local dealers, and they can arrange overnight delivery for a small premium.

WHAT SOFTWARE DO YOU NEED?

Desktop publishing can be done profitably with four types of programs, drawing, page layout, photo manipulation, and presentation. More advanced publishers may wish to venture into the exciting realm of multi-media, but that's another book. Naturally there are many programs that perform these functions but we have chosen our five favorites. None of the five are the least expensive on the market, but like hardware, you will quickly become discouraged with bargain software.

1. Aldus FreeHand is an excellent drawing program. It allows the beginner to create simple charts and graphs that can be exported to page layout programs. As you become more proficient you can create logotypes and other complex two dimensional art. Very soon you will amaze yourself by creating complex three dimensional illustrations. *FreeHand* also handles type beautifully, not like a page layout program but one paragraph at a time. This is a great application for signs (we'll talk more about this later) or flyers where type is isolate to one page and is secondary to an illustration. A similar program is Adobe Illustrator. Both programs retail for about $399 to $500 and can be ordered through mail order discounters.

drawing programs

2. Of the many page layout programs on the market, two enjoy the greatest international acceptance. *Aldus Pagemaker* and *Quark ExPress* are standards of the industry. Page layout programs are the core of the desktop business and it's important to choose a program that is widely accepted. Many cheeper programs have the same features, but it will become difficult to exchange files with printers and service bureaus, both here and abroad if they are unfamiliar with your software. Output to high resolution image-setters (Linotronic, Heil, etc.) can also be a problem with less familiar programs. As desk-top techniques become more widespread you will be able to shop the international market for the best price to out-put and print your documents if they are composed in widely accepted software (more about this later too).

page layout programs

Pagemaker seems to be the most intuitive of these two programs and is therefore preferred by front-end operators (designers). *XPress* has superior print-drivers (the part of the program that tells a high resolution out-put device what to out-put) and is therefore preferred by service bureaus and printers with out-put facilities. If you expect to send complex documents to a variety of service bureaus, *ExPress* will be your best choice. However, if your work will be out-put primarily in your own office and one local bureau *Pagemaker* will be easier to learn and manage. Both programs retail for about $599 to $699 and can be ordered through mail order discounters.

presentation programs

3. Aldus Persuasion is the industry standard for presentation programs. It assists you in the composition of slide or over-head transparency programs buy allowing you to import and manipulate text and graphics from other sources. You place these elements in a program matrix which can be edited and manipulated. Most service bureaus are equipped to out-put slides and over-head transparencies from *Persuasion*.

This can be a valuable source of income for the publisher-designer who is willing to spend the considerable time required to become proficient with *Persuasion*. Many small to mid-sized companies disparately need potent sales and marketing presentations that will distinguish them from the competition. Architects, planners and engineers need presentations that will help them acquire multi-million dollar contracts. Although not a primary source of income, these presentations can add handsomely to the publisher's bottom line. *Persuasion* is available from mail order discounters for as little as $325.

photo manipulation

4. PhotoShop is our final recommendation. It is an image manipulation program that allows you to do strange and wonderful things with photos. The best news is, its free! That is, if you take our recommendation on the purchase of a scanner. The Microteck 2 scanner comes packaged with the full version of *PhotoShop*. Be careful, many other scanners claim to include *PhotoShop* but you get an abbreviated version that does little more than run the scanner itself. You want the full version with all the features!

The down-side of owning a scanner with *PhotoShop* is that you will find yourself spending many unprofitable hours doctoring your personal photos and those of your friends. You can restore damaged or poorly exposed photos. You can take yourself out of a family reunion photo and put yourself in a Paris street scene. You can make your mate look younger and thinner and his/her parents older and uglier. In short, it's a great video game with an obvious business application. You can also save an important project and acquire many more by fixing a client's imperfect photos. *PhotoShop* is available from mail order discounters for $548.

FONTS

Probably the most important publishing software are the type *families vs faces* fonts you will be using in on your pages. A font is the designation given by a type publisher for a group of type. For instance, Stone is a type *family*, it contains three type *faces;* Stone Serif, Stone Sans and Stone Informal. Stone Sans comes in several type *weights* such as Stone Sans Light Stone Sans Book, Stone Sans Medium, Stone Sans Semi-bold and Stone Sans Bold. The type publisher (they used to be called foundries when type was cast in lead or steal) may designate and entire family as a font or just one face, or even part of a face. It all depends on how complex the type family is and how generous the publisher feels that day. The point is, don't expect to get every weight and style option when you purchase one font.

There are many fine type publishers in the market but Adobe is *Adobe* probably still the most pervasive in terms of library size (number of faces available) and technology. Others include Monotype, Bitstream, The Font Company and Image Club. You will find their mail order ads in *MacUser* and *MacWorld* magazines as well as in all the other popular design periodicals.

floppies vs CD ROM   There are basically two ways to buy fonts. You may purchase them one at a time on floppy disks from your local software dealer. This can be economical enough if you expect to use relatively few fonts and tail- or your business toward the low-end "word processing" market. However, you may find it inconvenient and expensive if you anticipate using many fonts and pursuing the high-end design business. The fact is, many publishers make a decent living supplying word processing and simple page layout, never using fonts other than those that were supplied with their system.

But the high paying jobs will require you to provide a wider range of type. This means you will want to invest in a compact disk pack- age. Many type publishers offer these packages which usually consist of a CD (looks just like the ones you use at home to play music), a CD ROM player (no, your home player won't work) and access codes to unlock some of the fonts contained on the disk. If you want addi- tional fonts from the library you simply call the publisher's toll free number, give them your order (and your credit card number) and they will give you an access code which allows you to take the font off the disk you already own ... a neat trick, yes? Most of these pack- ages are very good values because the publisher usually sells the CD ROM player at (or very near) their cost to get you to buy their fonts. Serious publishers will find many other uses for the players. They can help you access a wealth or research material now being presented on disks plus vast libraries of clip-art and clip photography.

clip art - clip photos   Clip-art has been around for years. It is essentially drawings, il- lustrations, designs and photos you can incorporate in your work quickly and easily, and without having to commission an illustrator or photographer to generate a custom work. For years publishers have sold books of clip art, which of course can be scanned into your page layout document. But now many of these same publishers are pro- viding clip art on disk, thus saving you the time and effort of scan- ning. The range of work is truly amazing and growing daily. It en- compasses everything from mediocre black and white spot illustration to detailed navigational maps to very fine color photography. Some publishers simply sell you their disk with the right to use anything on it. Others give you screen representations of the work and require you to purchase access codes to get the printer version of the image (allows the image to print). Many of the same publisher that sell type also sell clip art. The back pages of computer publishing magazines are filled with ads for clip art packages.

DEVELOPING A BUSINESS STRATEGY

Desktop publishing businesses can be divided in two major groups;

1. those that work on assignment and
2. those that generate original material for advertising or resale.

By far the easiest and least capital intensive is the **work on assignment** business. Conversely, a firm publishing original material has fewer limits on their earning potential.

ASSIGNMENT PUBLISHING

Most assignment publishers assemble a portfolio of work and present it to perspective clients. The clients offer assignments which are usually billed at the publisher's hourly rate. Sometimes a client will insist that a firm price be established for a project before it is begun. This means the publisher must guess at the number of hours they will spend on the job and structure their price accordingly.

The problem with assignment business is that publishers have a limited number of hours to sell (no one wants to work 24 hour a day). Presentations, routine office work and invoicing take a bite out of billable hours. Therefore, you are left with a finite number of hours for which you can bill.

You may solve this problem, in part, by hiring production employees at a relatively low rate and concentrating your time on sales *employees* and administration. This will expand your billable hours to some extent. However, employees can be expensive and add substantial administrative burdens. The added cost of equipment, office space, benefits and taxes reduces each new employee's billable productivity and once you have an employee you must work hard to keep them busy or face the distasteful chore of laying them off.

Subcontractors are usually a better solution. You can form a net- *subcontractors* work with other publishers in your area that work with similar equipment and software. Although you will have to pay them a higher hourly rate, you will not have to provide them with equipment, fringe benefits, office space or supplies. Because they are not employees, they handle all their own taxes and you should never have to pay them for an hour that you can't re-bill to your client.

Another benefit of networking with subcontractors is their ability *account ownership* to feed you work when your business is slow. Negotiate your retail rate (what you charge the end user) and wholesale rate (what you charge other publishers) in advance. Be certain your subcontractors understands who "owns the account" and have them agree never to contact your client directly unless you instruct them to do so. Stealing accounts should be grounds for dropping an individual from the network, thus cutting off future assignments. There are enough accounts for everyone if we prospect creatively.

DOCUMENTATION PUBLISHING

Try documentation publishing for software companies and soft- *software* ware end users. Although the software you will use is sold on the *docummentation* mass market in thousands of units, many companies and individuals are engaged in producing "limited edition software" tailored to the needs of smaller markets or even one user. Many large retailers, manufacturers, banks and other businesses commission programmers to write custom software specifically for their needs. The weakest part of this custom or limited edition software is usually the documentation.

Although the software itself is usually very sophisticated, it is useless until it can be understood and employed by everyone in the company, frequently even clerical level employees.

users groups　　Producing attractive documentation and training tools for this software can be a challenging and rewarding assignment. Most software or software revision projects are well funded. This means you can charge your full rate if you get your proposal in early in the project (before the programmers have eaten up all the budget). Contact local independent programmers. They usually have a resource network listed in the phone book as a Users Group (either IBM Users Group or Macintosh Users Group). Also contact the EDP department (electronic data processing department) of large and mid-sized companies in your area. Ask if they are anticipating changes in their operating systems in the future and how they are coping with documentation.

Don't worry, it is unlikely you will be required to actually write the documentation. That is done by the programmers. You may offer to translate the document to English. Most programmers failed English several times before resorting to programming. You will need to demonstrate the ability to grasp concepts and break them down into learnable units. The ability to generate simple graphs and illustrations (usually in *FreeHand* or *Illustrator*) is also important.

A problem faced by all publishers and designers is the typical client's inability to understand that skills are transferable from one job to another. If you can produce a legal brief with complex charts and graphs you can probably produce software documentation with charts and graphs. Clients are seldom able to make that quantum leap of faith. They want to see examples of their type of assignment in your portfolio. This leads to the age old dilemma, "how do I get a job without experience . . . how do I get experience without a job." One solution might be to volunteer to work with a budding young programmer for a very low (one time) rate. In return, you will get the experience, several copies of the document produced, and hopefully, a good recommendation and more work at normal rate. Failing this type of arrangement you might consider improving a few pages of documentation from off-the-shelf software. Unfortunately, it isn't difficult to find second-rate documentation. You could even show prospective clients the "before and after." Prior to your presentation, make certain your prospect didn't personally write the "before" example.

LEGAL PUBLISHING

Large law firms specializing in corporate law and anti-trust litigation are excellent prospects for publishers. Conversely, small law firms consisting of one or two principles or lawyers in private practice can usually provide little more than typing assignments at minimal rates. The larger firms need to prepare a wide variety of documents that often include charts and illustrations. There is usually an office manager/paralegal in charge of producing these documents. Ask for them when you call, not one of the principles. Again, it always helps to have examples of legal documentation. But if you don't, ask the office manager if they will allow you to reformat an obscure document from their files to demonstrate your skill.

In legal publishing you will be dealing with confidential and sensitive information. It is particularly important that you project an image of discrete dependability.

PROFIT FROM COPIES

Legal publishing offers additional opportunities for profit because most documents you generate (and possibly some you don't) will need to be copied several times, quickly. You'll find that an investment in a high speed copier can pay big dividends (the little desktop models won't do the volume needed here). Cannon, Minolta, Xerox and Kodak all make systems capable of the speed and volume required by large law firms. Look for a system designed to produce 40,000 impressions per month or more. The cost may seem high but a simple profit and loss proforma will demonstrate that you can easily *shopping for copiers* pay for the machine and make a handsome profit over the five to ten year life of the unit. You need only look at the number of copy shops that have sprung up recently to understand that this is a lucrative business. You will be offering a special advantage because you can produce the document and copy it at one location.

You can expect to pay anywhere from $26,000.00 for a low end machine to over $100,000.00 for a top-of-the-line Xerox. Granted, this is a capital intensive business not suited to the faint of heart. But, it can be a highly profitable adjunct to a desktop operation.

collators Your copier must have a collator feature. The bin type collator is best, even though it occupies more floor space. A stapler feature is valuable but not essential. The most important feature of any copier is the service contract. Check with every major dealer or manufacturer's rep in your area. Ask for price proposals on their models that fit your requirements. Then ask about their service policy. Is their service staff on call 24 hours a day, seven days a week? Much of your work will *service contracts* necessarily be done late nights and on weekends. What is their turn-around policy? Will they guarantee to get you up and running in four hours? Contracting for high volume copy services with only one machine is a little risky. Most shops have at least two machines for back-up. But a good reliable service staff that is committed to keeping you up and running can make a one machine shop viable.

subcontracting Don't be hesitant about taking on more volume than you can handle. The essence of the copy business is volume. Strike a deal with local copy shops to handle your overflow. This is a particularly good technique if you can accurately forecast the volume and timing of this overflow. Local shops will often keep operators on late shifts at lower than normal rates. They look at it as "plus business" or business that requires little incremental expense. You may only make $1/4$ to $1/2$ cent per impression on jobs you subcontract, but on 500 copies of a 40 page document, that's $50 to $100.

A copy shop's profits are made on fractions of cents, multiplied thousands of times. In most urban centers copying is a very competitive business. Therefore, it is essential you know precisely what your costs are at all times. Many copier companies state their proposals in ways that make it difficult for the customer to accurately compare prices or determine their exact costs. The cost of running a high speed copier must include: 1. toner (dry ink) 2. guaranteed maintenance program, including all parts 3. equipment purchase or lease 4. paper. One company may quote a price "per impression + supplies + maintenance." What does that mean? Actually it means nothing! Let perspective dealers know early in the negotiation that you only want to discuss inclusive per-impression costs . . . everything except paper. Tell them they must guarantee your total per-impression cost will not fluctuate over the term of the contract.

pricing and profit

For the more adventuresome, or mechanically inclined, the purchase of a used or reconditioned copier at auction can reduce your over head and give you an important edge over your competition. Check your local newspaper's classified "printers" or "business equipment " column. But be sure you can get service on any equipment you plan to purchase. Many copiers are dirt cheep because parts and service are no longer available.

used equipment

By far, the bulk of your customers will want simple white 24# stock. Buy it by the box (10 reams) or pallet (if you can handle that quantity) from wholesale sources such as Office Depot, Viking Office Supplies, The Price Club. These sources offer the most attractive prices and (in most locations) second day delivery.

paper and supplies

PROFESSIONAL'S PRESENTATIONS

Every day thousands of architects, structural engineers, and civil engineers compete for multi-million dollar contracts in both the public and private sectors of the economy. Each time a competition is announced by a government agency or private corporation these professionals are required to prepare a specific document detailing their

RFQ responses

suitability for the job, previous experience, the resources and budget they would devote to the job and the compensation they would require if selected to do the job. Although more than 12 copies of these presentations are seldom produced, much time and effort is lavished on the design, illustration and production. The core of most presentations is a bound book, it may also include video or multi-media segments.

This is an area of opportunity for the more sophisticated publisher, capable of combining photography, well edited copy and illustration in a slick, well designed package. It is also an ideal application for the Cannon color copier, (mentioned earlier).

Full color pages can be composed using your scanner and either *FreeHand* or a page layout program. Scan photos that will be reduced in size at a resolution of about 150 dots per inch. This will keep the files from getting so large they become unmanageable. Scan all photos that will be enlarged on the page at 300 d.p.i. to preserve clarity. Add your text and any charts or graphs, background graphics, rules or format devices and have your service bureau output your pages. Use a waxer or spray mount adhesive to mount the pages back to back with a sheet of 65# vellum bristol sandwiched in the center. Bind the pages with a comb or Wire-O binding system.

use of large formats   You can give your presentation added punch by formatting it on 11" x 17" sheets. These are especially effective when used horizontally so when the book is opened it occupies a full 34" x 11" on the recipient's desk (try ignoring that presentation). Because the Cannon Laser Printer won't actually print edge-to-edge on the sheet you may wish to trim off the 1/4" white margin so your color appears to bleed the page. Otherwise, you may simply use this white area as a design feature. Gives your Wire-O or comb bound presentation professional polish by adding a small colored stripe along the gutter side of each page, the left side of the front cover and the right side of the back cover. The stripe should match the color of the binding material you plan to use and after it is trimmed to bleed the page the stripe should be about 1/8" wider than the diameter of the binding material. This will make the binding look more like a part of the book, rather than an after-thought.

A recent advance in the laser color technology has come from *Xerox color* Xerox with the introduction of their new color copier. The advantage of the Xerox model is it's ability to handle up to 8.5" x 11", 65# cover stock and therefore to print on both sides of the page. Because the Cannon machine can only out-put the equivalent of 70# text stock (65# text is actually lighter than 65# cover) it can not print on both sides of the page. The Cannon melts the toner (dry ink) from the first side impression as it tries to deposit the second side impression, thus creating a gummed-up mess in the fusser drum. The heavier paper used by he Xerox machine provides just enough insulation to prevent this, provided the toner deposit on the first side is not to heavy. Unfortunately, the Xerox won't consistently handle 11" x 17" cover stock . . . well may be some day.

BINDING ADDS PROFIT

Speaking of binding, you can make added profit with only a modest investment if you offer to bind your client's documents. There are several systems available to the desktop market ranging from simple post binding to perfect binding in a Morocco leather case.

VeloBind makes a simple plastic post system that retails for about *VeloBind* $100 (as low as $50 from discounters) including basic supplies. The result is fine for internal reports and the books can be dressed up by using more interesting cover stocks from your art supply store, but it is far from a "prestige" look. It's other drawback is that it is limited in thickness to 25 pages of 24# bond.

The GBC 1 Step Binding System produces a glued book of up to 30 pages with 1/8" spine. It retails for $129 ($103.50 from discounters). This produces a product that looks somewhat like a perfect bound book you might buy in a retail store. The thickness is still a severe limitation.

comb binding   By far, the most widely accepted system is *comb binding* that consists of a 19 hole punch and a device that helps you insert a plastic comb through the holes. DuroBind makes a light-duty model that retails for $179.00 ($150 through discounters) plus supplies. It's an attractive device that occupies very little desk space. However, if you anticipate the need to bind more than 20 books a week you will be better served by an Ibico Deluxe machine. These are industry standards that retail for $556 ($399 from discounters) plus supplies.

padding   Padding is still another type of binding, except in this case the binding is designed to come apart. It is done by placing the sheets to be padded and a sheet of gray chip board in a padding vice. Padding compound, a liquid available in white and several colors, is applied sparingly to one edge of the stack and allowed to dry. Everything you need can be purchased from a printer's supply house for well under $100.00.

looseleaf binders   One of the most profitable binding systems will require little or no labor on your part. Sell your clients loose leaf binders. Loose leaf binders are the perfect solution for documents that may need to grow or change in the future and today there is wide range of sizes styles and qualities from which to choose. You can customize binders of all sizes with screen printing and embossing. The sealed "view binder" makes it possible to insert a full color photo or print in a clear pocket on the front, back and spine of a binder then heat-seal the pockets to create an attractive, permanent and durable unit. Check the resource list for manufacturers. You should have no difficulty selling binders at a 30% markup (130% of your cost plus freight).

ALL THE WORLD LOVES A BROCHURE

Probably the single largest print advertising media is the brochure. It is used by large and small businesses alike.

If you live near a resort area there are dozens of motels, hotels, attractions, restaurants and amusements that require brochures. Most resort areas have a chamber of commerce or association responsible for the area's promotion. Contact them for a list of members. Such an association may need a brochure itself and frequently has standard specifications for its member's brochures so they can be placed in the association's direct mail offers and local take-one holders. Offer the association a special rate on their brochure in return for their recommendation to the membership. Offer association members a special rate in return for mention in their newsletter, then offer to publish their newsletter.

resort market

Most resort brochures are three to four panel (six to eight page) folded sheets, designer to fit a counter-top holder or vest pocket. Practically all are full color, unless the budget is extremely tight. The most practical way to produce a short run of brochures is through a *gang printer*. These are large printing houses that place small jobs together on the same press run to give you some of the economies of a large run. One of the best, although not always the cheapest, is McGrew Color Graphics in Kansas City (resource guide). Write to them for their video tape and dealer's kit. They do an extremely good job of supporting desktop professionals who sell their products.

gang printers

When you receive McGrew's package you will be delighted to find that they also produce many other products of interest to the resort industry including postcards. Why not sell a batch of postcards at the same time you are selling a brochure? You might even consider a special package rate for the client who commits to both at the same time.

postcard sales

Another add-on profit source is the brochure holder. These are clear plastic stands that hold the brochures neatly on a counter top.

brochure holders

They are available from Seigal Displays (resource guide) and can easily be sold at a 30% mark-up. Remember, you won't get rich from any single sale, but the successful publisher takes advantage of every profit opportunity.

sell sheets or catalog sheets

Small manufacturing firms and wholesalers also need brochures. Because they are more frequently used as hand-outs at trade shows, the industrial brochure usually takes the form of an 8 1/2" x 11" flyer or *sell-sheet*. These can be full color on one side and black and white on the second side or full color two sides. They may be printed on 80# text or 10 to 12 point cover stock depending on the client's budget and desire to make a quality impression. A more elaborate sell sheet is made by folding an 11" x 17" sheet to create a four page 8 1/2" x 11" presentation. Sell sheets work best when they are used to promote one item or a closely related group of items. They are, in effect, mini-catalogs.

press kit catalogs

Sell sheets comprise a large portion of most gang printers volume, thus they usually have excellent prices on this item and can produce them quickly and in relatively low quantities. A good way to build your own business volume is to target the small wholesaler who doesn't believe he can afford a bound catalog. Show him how you can build a catalog for him over a period of time by producing sell-sheets on his various products. Eventually, he will want a two pocket press-kit or loose leaf binder in which he can present his collection of sell-sheets. Although this is a more expensive way to produce a catalog, it gives the client the flexibility to add or drop items from his line without reprinting an entire book. This can be a lifesaver for the small start-up business and you can profit handsomely.

THE STAR OF PUBLISHING . . . THE CATALOG

Once you and your client have mastered the sell-sheet, it's just a hop skip and a jump to the catalog. Well, not really. Where sell sheets impose their own kind of discipline by virtue of their limited size, catalogs (even short 16 page catalogs) require extreme client-publisher discipline. One of the most important benefits of publishing a catalog is that the client comes away with a much more focused view of his business. Most entrepreneurs should probably plan to do a catalog, even if they never print it because it forces them to look at their business in an orderly way.

A good catalog is developed by analyzing a business, deciding what products (or services) contribute what percent of volume to the bottom line and then allotting space based on profit contribution. The businessperson may choose to skew the allotments in favor of products he feels should be up-trending or have greater future potential, but there must be a relationship between product volume (or anticipated volume) and space allotment.

prepare catalog by analizing business

Hay! isn't this supposed to be art?
Why are you letting the businessman plan his book?

Art my foot! If you are asking someone to spend several thousand dollars you had better create a book that produces tangible results for your client. It's interesting to note that many major retailers actually sell the pages of their direct mail catalogs by the square inch to their vendors. That's right, Calvin Klein actually pays Macys or Daytons to be in many of their best-selling books.

assign space by profit contribution

Every aspect of the catalog should be approached in the same objective manner. The answer to these questions will determine the form and content of the catalog:

questions that determin catalog format

1. Is the customer interested in the photos or is data more important?
2. Does the customer want breadth of selection or do too many choices jeopardize the sale?
3. How can we make it easy for the customer to respond to our offer?
4. Is price an important factor or is prestige more important?
5. Are subtle details, requiring multiple views of one item, important selling points? Can diagrams show details more effectively?

6. Can copy explain important features not obvious in photos?

7. Can tables be used to dramatize the superiority of a product over it's competition?

8. Can old photos be reworked in another way to create a sense of newness at minimal expense?

9. Does the catalog promote an image of industry leadership for your client?

10. Does the overall book, including stock, design and photography (or illustration) relate well to the target market?

tools for catalog organization

Beyond allowing the client's needs to dictate the form of their book, organization is the essence of catalog creation, organization in every sense. When you create a catalog you are organizing data in the most effective way possible. If you can't organize a complex project you can't organize an other man's business, and to a large degree that is exactly what you are doing.

The basic tools of catalog organization are:

1. The proposal
2. The space allotment mock-up
3. The production time-line
4. The progress report.

proposal contracts

Every time a publisher enters into an agreement to produce a work, for which they will not be paid immediately, they must execute a written contract with their client. This contract protects both the publisher and the client by clearly defining the roll each will play in the project. The contract we prefer is an adaptation of the proposal form suggested by the National Association of Graphic Artists. We have made three important changes in the form which has been included in the appendix.

First, we have opened with a brief introduction that explains what we do and how we charge for it. This is covered again in the fine print, but we feel it is just more friendly to explain to the uninitiated businessperson (which most clients are) what they can expect. By stating this in very positive terms we actually use the introduction as an opportunity to promote ourselves. After all, the client has usually not made a commitment at this point.

Second, we have added a line which the client must initial before signing the proposal. It clearly states that the proposal is for specific services. When additional services (including revisions) are requested they will be performed at prevailing rates. The client will be kept advised of the progress of work and the amount of increase in project costs necessitated by requested additions (or revisions). It is very important that the client understand that a proposal reflects the number of hours a publisher believes is necessary to complete a project without revisions. No publisher (I know) is clairvoyant. If they were they would probably be investment councilors. It is impossible to foresee how many hours of changes or revisions a client will require in a project. You must politely inform the client that you will happily do whatever pleases them . . . But the meter is ticking!

defining limits of the job

Yes, you will get resistance on this point. But, if a client withholds a project because you can not give them an absolute cap on expenses before beginning, then the job wasn't worth having. Assurance of constant and open communication with he client is the best way to overcome his objections on this point. It is not uncommon for a catalog to cost twice the initial proposal price. You must assure the client you can produce the work for the price you propose barring changes in specification.

Finally, we have included a set of printer's terms. The terms most widely used by designers do not sufficiently cover printing industry standard practices and conventions. As you may have guessed by now, much of our income is derived by brokering the printing of our projects. Therefore our customers must be acquainted with these additional terms.

A word of caution; when working with a new client, be very specific in the project description. Place limits on the design and mechanical hours, number of photos, graphs, illustrations and color separations. Vague proposals lead to misunderstandings and unpaid invoices.

the paper mock-up   The very best way to lay out a catalog, even in this age of computer programs, is to cut paper to the size of two page spreads, fold it in half and create a physical mock-up. To spite the claims of software publishers, there is still no better way to make catalog decisions than by looking at an actual size mock-up. Using the space allotment decisions your client has given you, based on his volume analysis, begin to assign space in the mock-up. Draw the merchandise as it will appear on the pages. Very crude drawings will be fine. They will show you roughly how large your finished photos will be and give you an indication of how much space you can devote to copy. Indicate lines of copy with horizontal rules. Don't worry if the mock-up looks crude. It is only intended to describe the basic structure of the catalog. There will be plenty of time for refinement. Once you and your client have reviewed the mock-up and agreed on the basics of space allotment, tables, charts, copy treatment and other features, you may prepare the production schedule or time-line.

schedules   We have also enclosed a copy of our project schedule. You may also purchase software that generates a schedule or *critical-path* plan but we have found that this simple form, created in a word processing or page layout program works very well. It is easy to update, looks very professional and performs two essential tasks. It lets the client and those working on the project know what is expected and when. It also impress upon the client the need for their cooperation and lets them know that they are in the project's driver's seat. Most catalogs are timed to coincide with other events such as trade shows, product introductions or media campaigns. Therefore, late catalogs are nearly worthless catalogs. Just as it is imperative that your clients accept responsibility for cost over-runs, you must also place scheduling delays clearly in their court.

The final control document is the progress report. It is easy to prepare because it is a combination of the proposal and schedule. You may simply copy sections from each and up-date them as needed. We suggest you do this weekly if possible, bi-weekly is the minimum requirement. We usually fax it to the client and ask that they confirm it by signing and faxing back the last page. Yes, it looks like a lot of work but it's worth it. It is so much easier than suing a client for cost over-runs (months after a job is delivered) that we never give it a second thought. We build the time it takes to generate the report into all complex projects.

progress report

GENERATING PHOTOGRAPHY

One thorny issue for most desktop publishers is the cost of generating good quality photography for brochures, sell-sheets and catalogs. Although the new technology has brought typesetting within the reach of almost everyone, good quality product photography has gotten progressively more expensive. Poor photos make poor brochures and poor brochures make unhappy clients. There is no way around it, you must have good photos to produce acceptable work. One of the most difficult things you will do (and you'll do it over and over), is explain to an enthusiastic low budget client why the out-of-focus snapshot he just got from the one-hour-processor won't work.

Most good commercial photographers working in or near urban centers charge between $1000 and $1200 per day, and they're worth every penny. Of course, this is just the beginning; there's $250 to $500 per day for film and processing, $70 to $120 per hour for models (plus 10% agency fee), site fees for the use of homes or locations, stylists at $350 to $550 a day to dress models or sets, and naturally $75 a day for a poor photographer's assistant. Although it's unlikely you'll be tackling a project this complex in your first year, a $5000 per day photo-shoot is not extravagant or unusual. We haven't even talked about lunch for the models and crew (you're expected to pay) and drayage and model transportation to the site.

commercial photographers

do-it-yourself photography   There are alternatives for the client and publisher on a limited budget. The first and best is you! If you have any interest whatsoever in photography you can turn this dilemma into a profit source for yourself. The new automatic cameras, like the Minolta 10000 do a great job in *available light* (meaning no artificial light). After a short course in their use (something that frequently comes with their purchase) you will be fully qualified to take decent shots of real estate, outdoor events or any product that can be reasonably shown in a bright outdoor setting. Bill your client half the prevailing rate for commercial photographers in your area and you will soon recoup your $1000. investment in camera, lens (get a good zoom lens 28mm to 100mm) and tripod.

using supplier's photos   Encourage your client to ask his suppliers for photography. It's amazing how many products are photographed two and three times, once by the manufacturer, once by the distributor, and again by the retailer. Why?

clip or stock photos   If your client's business is concept, rather than product, oriented you might consider the use of stock photography. Our resource section list several good stock photo houses that rent very fine shots that apply to a variety of businesses. Write to each on your letterhead requesting a catalog. The trick to working with a stock house is in negotiating low usage rates. Each photo is rented for a specific project and the rent depends on the usage. The higher the exposure, the longer the press run, the higher the rate. Deal honestly but don't inflate the importance of the photos to your project when describing your usage to the agent. Most stock houses are very happy to place small contracts for their contributing photographers.

wedding or portrait photographers   Check the yellow pages for portrait photographers. Many independent portrait photographer, especially young ones, make very acceptable candid and fashion photographers. Ask to see a portfolio of work. If you see dozens of stayed studio shots, all lit the same way, simply say, "very nice" and excuse yourself. On the other hand, if you see some evidence of flair and personality in the work you may have stumbled onto pay dirt. Most portrait photographers are delighted to work for $600 (about half the commercial rate) a day and will do their own styling.

Some larger urban centers have high volume production studios *high volume studios* that will grind out acceptable product photos for much less than a custom photographer's day rate. Don't expect miracles, but the work will probably be well lit and in focus. Keep your layouts precise clean and simple and you won't be disappointed.

If you must use a custom commercial photographer negotiate! Very few are busy all the time. Everyone can use "fill-in work" to take up those slack hours. If you and your client can plan carefully and have enough time to schedule the shoot over several weeks you can easily negotiate a better rate. Nothing runs up a bill faster than a "rush."

RETAIL SIGNS AND POSTERS

One source of profitable work most desktop publishers fail to rec- *retailer's sign shops* ognize is signage and posters and one of the largest users of such paper signs is your local retailer. Most retailers are aware of the many studies showing that they can generate substantially greater volume in a given product if customers are presented with a well composed, easy to read signs listing the product's less obvious features. For this reason, large department stores have extensive sign shops that generate a variety of signs at the request of the buying staff. These sign shops once used mechanical devices that operated like large typewriters or flat bed proofing presses employing hand set cold type. Most now use much the same equipment you have to produce the most common size signs including; $5^1/_2$" x 7", 7" x 11", 8 $^1/_2$" x 11", 11" x 14",11" x 17" and 22" x 28".

Many sign shops have purchased desktop computer systems specifically adapted to sign production, however, your equipment will work just as well, if not better. Most of the signs listed above are generated on laser printer masters and duplicated in Xerox machines for branch store distribution. Few in-house sign shops have the capacity to deal with peek work loads and because many are run by highly paid union employees, overtime is expensive. This creates the ideal opportunity for the independent contractor, willing to offer fast turn-around service at a reasonable price. Most large retailers have a specific signing format and type face. Study the point of sale signs in your local department stores. Make a presentation of signs in those formats to demonstrate to the sign shop manager that you can create work exactly like that done in-house.

You may offer to produce masters only or if you have a copier, both masters and duplication. Your fees should include a one-time set up charge for each new format and size. Thereafter, they should be structured on a per-sign basis with a descending scale that rewards large orders placed at a single time. Although your rates must be adapted for your locality, typical rate sheet might look like this:

pricing signs   5 1/2" x 7" to 8 1/2" x 11" Horizontal - Housewares Format

Set-up Cost	$5.00
1 to 10 signs per order, 30 words or less	1.50 each master
11 to 20 signs per order	1.20 each master
21 to 30 signs per order	1.10 each master
31 to 50 signs per order	1.00 each master
50 to 100 signs per order	.90 each master

It is a good idea to reward all your clients for delivering as much work at one time as possible. Every time you have to stop one job and start another you loose valuable time and concentration.

sign duplication   Duplication is usually done on white 65# vellum bristol stock. Be sure to factor the labor cost required to trim the signs to size into your pricing. For instance, you will get two 5 1/2" x 7" signs from a single sheet of 8 1/2" x 11" stock but you will have to make two cuts to get them. Therefore, you should charge the same price for both sizes of copy. Base your duplication prices on the local market for such services, being sure you allow for the heavier weight paper.

Because you will purchase a laser printer capable of 11" x 17" stock, you will easily be able to accommodate posters up to that size. Many retailers and event planners will want larger posters or posters with multiple colors. This is relatively simple if you use your local service bureau to generate Cannon LaserColor® prints and employ a montague approach to constructing posters larger than 11" x 17".

One of the most popular poster sizes for retailers, hotels and event planners is 22" x 28". This is the size of half a sheet of colored poster board, available from your local art supply dealer. It fits the existing poster frames owned by these facilities. Simply compose a "type-panel" using the copy supplied by your client on the 11" x 17" sheet your laser printer can accommodate (or have it out-put in color on the Cannon LaserColor® copier). Keep in mind that this sheet will become a part of a larger layout. Purchase half sheets of poster board in an attractive color and apply your type-panel to the larger board. You can also use smaller pieces of contrasting colored paper and tape to highlight your design and make the type-panel appear more important.

posters for hotels and retailers

Many clients will need posters which include photographs of individuals who are making personal appearances. Frequently, the client will supply you with standard 8" x 10" glossy publicity shots which can be incorporated into your layout. If the client can't provide enough copies for the number of posters required you might offer to scan one copy into your layout and out-put it as part of the type panel through your laser printer or the Cannon LaserColor® copier (at a nominal added charge). Another option is to have your service bureau make direct color copies and apply them to the poster as you would a glossy print.

incorporating photos

51

waxers vs sprayglue   When composing a small quantity of posters you may use spray adhesive to hold the various elements to the poster board. But, if your poster business grows you will definitely want to consider the purchase of a large waxer. Spray glue is very difficult to control and should never be used near your computer, copier, or any delicate equipment. Always use a face mask when spraying and avoid extended use. Waxers, on the other hand, are clean, neat and easy to control. They come in a wide variety of sizes from small hand held models to large units capable of coating an 18" sheet of paper in one stroke. If you are serious about your poster business, buy the large, 18" size from a mail order discounter. It will cost about $650, but it will pay for itself quickly. Another advantage of wax adhesive over spray glue is that your elements are more easily positioned and repositioned. Waxed elements don't stick until they are rubbed down with a roller.

pricing posters   Custom posters can generate considerable income. The basic charge for a 22" x 28" poster should be no less than $45 each and might go much higher for more complex designs. Rush service charges for orders required in less that 48 hours should also apply. Check your local market for other's rush charge policy, but 100% surcharge for 24 hour service and 50% surcharge for 36 hour service is well within reason. You will find these surcharges will seldom deter clients who genuinely need your service. Actually, a $45 poster with a 100% rush charge will cost the client just slightly more than the standard rates charges by flat-bed press (cold type) sign shops. If you are working in a small community where your only competition is a flat-bed press operator or hand letterer you may want to consider establishing higher rates for all your work.

screen printed mats   Another source for poster profits is the custom mat. Offer to create a screen printed mat for your consistent clients such as retailers and hotels. Design an simple but attractive boarder that incorporates the company's logo. You may have a local screen printer reproduce a three month supply in two or three colors, usually including the company's corporate colors. Keep the supply in your office but bill the client for the entire order up front. As poster orders come in you will find the mat simplifies your job and makes the 11" x 17" type panel look more like an integral part of the poster design. The client will appreciate the customized look of his work.

Finally, you might even consider investment in a vinyl cutting system to supplement your sign making capability. There are several systems currently marketed, some are self contained machines that include the three elements of cut vinyl systems; the computer, the software and the plotter. Since you already have a computer, the purchase of a self contained system would be redundant. Besides, they start at about $10,000 and you would have to be very serious about sign making to justify that investment.

plotter cut vinyl signs

There are, however, several companies promoting software packages that allow your computer to interface with a plotters thus producing a very acceptable vinyl cutting system. A plotter is a printing device, originally developed to create architectural and engineering drawings for a program called **CAD (computer assisted design)**. Most plotters have sprocket drive wheels which allow it to move tractor drive paper, drafting mylar or other materials both backward and forward under a drawing pen. The pen can move from left to right at the same time the material is being moved backward and forward. These two simultaneous motions, controlled by a very sophisticated program are capable of precise drawings.

It wasn't long before some clever engineer substituted a fine knife blade for the drawing pen and pressure sensitive vinyl for paper and gave birth to a whole new industry, vinyl signs. At first it seemed like a great idea. Conventionally lettered signs were expensive and time consuming to prepare. Vinyl could be cut in large sheets (up to 60" in large commercial shops) and applied to virtually any substrate (surface). Hand lettering was a thing of the past. The problem is that it was too good an idea. Everybody jumped on the band wagon at once and the wagon collapsed. Promoters quickly packaged franchised business and sold ten to every small town. It would be amazing if one of these store-front sign shops hasn't opened (and closed) near you.

If you should live in one of the five markets not yet over-saturated by sign shops, and/or your customers have expressed an interest in on-going sign contracts. You might consider investing about $6500 in a modest vinyl sign system. That's about what it will cost to purchase the software and a reasonable plotter, plus a basic supply of vinyl. *Signs Of The Times* and *Sign Business* are two trade magazines that are full of offers of systems. The best system we have found, assuming you have followed our other hardware and software suggestions is the Sign Post™ sign cutting connection for the Macintosh by Taylored Graphics, P.O. Box 1900, Freedom, California. Under no circumstances should you buy a franchise. There are too many out there and the chance of another franchise (another company with virtually the same product) opening next door is not remote. Frankly, if you exploit a few of the other suggestions we have made, sticking vinyl to plywood construction barricades will seem less appealing.

CHOOSING A PAPER TO FIT YOUR JOB

Today designers can choose from a vast array of domestic and imported papers. Your local wholesale distributor will be glad to help you select your stock and provide samples.

Offset printing stock is calibrated in weight by pounds and divided into the following categories:

Uncoated text stock is available in weights from 40# to 150#. It is usually white, but occasionally found in off white shades. Its primary use is for inexpensive books and magazines.

Uncoated cover stock is available in weights from 50# to 130#. It is stiffer than comparable weight text stock and comes in a wider range of colors and textures. It is used for book covers, greeting cards and announcements, business cards and other applications where more substantial stock is a requirement.

Coated text stock is available in the same range of weights as uncoated text. Coatings are applied to the sheet to give it a mat or gloss surface. Both surfaces tend to hold the ink more effectively than uncoated stock and improve the rendition of fine detail and halftones. Coated stocks are used for higher quality books, magazines and direct mail advertisements.

Coated cover stock is available in the same weights as uncoated stock and used for quality book covers and postcards.

Castcoated stocks come in both text and cover weights and have an exceptionally high gloss surface suited to fine quality printing.

Bond is primarily used for business correspondence and forms. It is available in weights from 13# to 32# and a variety of qualities and finishes. The least expensive bond is called sulphite. Its primary use is in copiers and for instant printing. Better quality bonds contain various percentages of cotton fiber. Generally, higher cotton content indicates finer quality. Most fine bond sheets are available in both wove and laid finishes. The wove sheet is a flat paper lacking any distinctive grain. The laid sheet has a subtle subsurface pattern.

Although the standard size of a sheet of paper is generally considered 8.5" x 11", most papers come from the mill in *master sheet* sizes ranging from 17.5" x 22.5" to 44" x 64". A printer may order the sheets at *mill size* or cut by the distributor to fit his press and the specific job run. With the exception instant printers, most jobs are run *several-up*. This means there are as many as 32 copies of the job on the press form being run at one time. After printing the master sheets are trimmed into the individual pages. This is how printers achieve a bleed effect. If the printer actually allowed ink to run off the page it would create an uncontrolled mess in the plant and contaminate the

THE DESKTOP IDEA BOOK

stock. The image area on a bleed page never comes more than 1/8 inch from the edge of the master sheet during the printing process, but it is **trimmed to bleed** after printing.

Choosing the right master sheet for each job can dramatically effect the cost of a printing job. Consult your printer or paper distributor to find the most cost effective sheet for each of your jobs.

The first impression your audience will receive from your printed page is often depends on your envelope. When your print order runs several hundred thousand you may choose to have custom envelopes *converted* or made up in your choice of stocks and custom colors. On short runs this can be rather costly and you should rely on stock envelope resources.

The 11 basic envelope styles are:

Commercial, the most popular, is a long horizontal with a rounded point closure flap on long edge. It is available in sulphite bond and some finer bonds in the following sizes:

#5	$3^1/_{16}$" x $5^1/_2$"	#6	$3 \ ^3/_8$" x 6"
#$6^1/_4$	$3 \ ^1/_2$" x 6"	#6 1/2	$3 \ ^9/_{16}$" x 6 $^1/_4$"
#$6^3/_4$	$3 \ ^5/_8$" x 6 $^1/_2$"	#7	$3 \ ^3/_4$" x 6 $^3/_4$"
#$7^1/_2$	$3 \ ^3/_4$" x 7 $^5/_8$"	#7 3/4 monarch	$3 \ ^7/_8$" x 7 $^1/_2$"
data card	$3 \ ^1/_2$" x 7 $^5/_8$"	#8 5/8 check	$3 \ ^5/_8$" x 8 $^5/_8$"
#9	$3 \ ^7/_8$" x 8 $^7/_8$"	#10	$4 \ ^1/_8$" x 9 $^1/_2$"
#$10^1/_2$	$4 \ ^1/_2$" x 9 $^1/_2$"	#11	$4 \ ^1/_2$" x $10^3/_8$"
#12	$4 \ ^3/_4$" x 11"		

Booklet envelopes are more square in shape with a less pointed closure flap on the longer edge. They are usually available in sulphite stocks in a limited color ranges. Their unique folding design allows printing on both front and back, making them popular in the direct mail advertising industry. They are available in the following sizes:

#2 $\frac{1}{2}$	4 $\frac{1}{2}$" x 5 $\frac{7}{8}$"	#3	4 $\frac{3}{4}$" x 6 $\frac{1}{2}$"
#4 $\frac{1}{4}$	5" x 7 $\frac{1}{2}$"	#4 $\frac{1}{2}$	5 $\frac{1}{2}$" x 7 $\frac{1}{2}$"
#5	5 $\frac{1}{2}$" x 8 $\frac{1}{2}$"	#6	5 $\frac{3}{4}$" x 8 $\frac{7}{8}$"
#6 $\frac{1}{2}$	6" x 9"	#6 $\frac{3}{4}$	6 $\frac{1}{2}$" x 9 1/2"
#7	6 $\frac{1}{4}$" x 9 $\frac{5}{8}$"	#7 $\frac{1}{4}$	7" x 10"
#7 $\frac{1}{2}$	7 $\frac{1}{2}$" x 10 $\frac{1}{2}$"	#8	8" x 11 $\frac{1}{8}$"
#8	$\frac{3}{4}$" x 11 $\frac{1}{2}$"	#9 $\frac{1}{2}$	9" x 12"
#10	9 $\frac{1}{2}$" x 12 $\frac{5}{8}$"	#13	10" x 13"
#14	5" x 11 $\frac{1}{2}$"		

Window envelopes are available in one and two window styles. The second window is for the return address. They are available in both white sulphite and brown craft stocks in the following sizes:

#6 $\frac{1}{4}$	3 $\frac{1}{2}$" x 6"	#6 $\frac{3}{4}$	3 $\frac{5}{8}$" x 6 $\frac{1}{2}$"
#7	3 $\frac{3}{4}$" x 6 $\frac{3}{4}$"	#7 $\frac{3}{4}$	3 $\frac{7}{8}$" x 7 $\frac{1}{2}$"
#8 $\frac{5}{8}$	3 $\frac{5}{8}$" x 8 $\frac{5}{8}$"	#9	3 $\frac{7}{8}$" x 8 $\frac{7}{8}$"
#10	4 $\frac{1}{8}$" x 9 $\frac{1}{2}$"	#11	4 $\frac{1}{2}$" x 11"
#12	4 $\frac{3}{4}$" x 11"	#14	5" x 11 $\frac{1}{2}$"

Remittance envelopes are like small booklet envelopes with an extra large closure flap than can often be removed and used as an order form or coupon. Their folding characteristics allow printing on both front and back surfaces. The are available in sulphite and some coated text stocks in the following sizes:

#6 $\frac{1}{4}$	3 $\frac{1}{2}$" x 6"	3 $\frac{3}{8}$" flap
#6 $\frac{1}{2}$	3 $\frac{1}{2}$" x 6 $\frac{1}{4}$"	3 $\frac{3}{8}$" flap
#6 $\frac{3}{4}$	3 $\frac{5}{8}$" x 6 $\frac{1}{2}$"	3 $\frac{1}{2}$" flap
#9	3 $\frac{7}{8}$" x 8 $\frac{7}{8}$"	

Policy envelopes are primarily used for insurance policies, bonds and mortgage documents. Their tall thin shape and the closure flap on the narrow end makes an unusual presentation that could be applied to direct mail. They are available in various stocks in the following sizes:

#9	4" x 9"	#10	4 1/8" x 9 1/2"
#11	4 1/4" x 10 3/8"	#12	4 3/4" x 10 7/8"
#14	5" x 11 1/2"		

Catalog envelopes are the standard manila envelopes we know from the stationery store. Today they come in a variety of stocks including bright colored cover stocks (from speciality converters and gift wholesalers), and tyveck, a synthetic "paper" highly resistant to tare and moisture damage. Basic size for catalog envelopes include:

#1	6" x 9"	#1$3/4$	6$1/2$" x 9$1/2$"
#2	6$1/2$" x 10"	#3	7" x 10"
#6	7$1/2$" x 10$1/2$"	#7	8" x 11"
#8	8 1/4" x 11$1/4$"	#9$1/2$	8$1/2$" x 10$1/2$"
#10$1/2$	9" x 12"	#12$1/2$	9$1/2$" x 12$1/2$"
#13$1/2$	10" x 13"	#14$1/4$	11$1/4$" x 14$1/4$"
#14$1/2$	11$1/2$" x 14$1/2$"		

Announcement text envelopes come in the widest range of text stocks, color coordinated with finer uncoated card and text stocks. They are primarily used for greeting cards, invitations and announcements. Their construction is similar to a booklet envelope with a square closure flap. The edge of the flap is often deckled (roughly cut) to give a hand made impression. They are available in the following sizes:

#A-2	4$3/8$" x 5$5/8$"	#A-6	4$3/4$" x 6$1/2$"
#A-7	5$1/4$" x 7$1/4$"	#A-8	5$1/2$" x 8$1/8$"
#A-10	6$1/4$" x 9$5/8$"	Slim	3$7/8$" x 8$7/8$"

Wallet Flap envelopes are a heavier version of the commercial envelope. They have a deeper flap and are usually a much heavier paper for use with bulky correspondence. The are available in the following sizes:

#10	$4^1/_8$" x $9^1/_2$"	#11	$4^1/_2$" x $10^3/_8$"
#12	$4^3/_4$" x 11"	#14	5" x $11^1/_2$"
#16	6" x 12"		

Baronial envelopes are more square than commercials with long pointed flaps. They are used like announcement envelopes, for greetings and social occasions but they are generally available in a only bond (stationery) stocks in the following sizes:

#2	$3^3/_{16}$" x $4^1/4$"	#4	$3^5/_8$" x $4^5/_8$"
#5	$4^1/_8$" x $5^1/_8$"	#$5^1/_4$	$4^1/_4$" x $5^1/_4$"
#$5^1/_2$	$4^3/_8$" x $5^5/_8$"	#$5^3/_4$	$4^1/_2$" x $5^3/_4$"
#6	5" x 6"		

As noted earlier, virtually any size or shape envelope may be converted from any stock as long as you are prepared to pay a premium or place a large minimum order. Designers who want large areas of bleed ink coverage will even have their stock printed first, then turned into envelopes. This is necessary because,as we mentioned before, printers can not bleed ink in the printing process, sheets must be trimmed to bleed after printing. Envelopes are also more difficult to print because of their multiple layers of stock and seams. Smaller presses will allow only minimal ink coverage on commercial type envelopes.

NICKELS AND DIMES

resumes

You may be disappointed that we haven't devoted three volumes to letterheads and resumes. Sorry. Yes, we have all done them at one time or another. When business is slow you do what you can. But instead of wasting your time on busy-work you should go out and land a big software documentation account or a forms-design account for a major bank. Small jobs for individuals just don't pay. If your idea of life in the fast lane is $20,000 annually, fine. Do your resumes for $30 each (about all the market will bare). With the interview, typing and revisions each resume will take about 90 minutes. That's five per day (if you had clients lined up down the hall). That's $160 a day or $40,000 a year.

Well, $40,000 doesn't sound so bad. But you'll still never make it with resumes. Consider all the time you'll spend promoting your service, doing your books, trying to collect from your friends who think they are doing you a favor by letting you practice on their resume. Small jobs produce small returns. The cost of setting up each file, handling small amounts of money and dealing with hundreds of individuals will quickly eat up your profits and nerves.

short-run brochures and stationery
Several paper companies are promoting preprinted laser papers that allow you to generate designy color brochures and newsletters through your laser printer. They say this is a great concept for clients who only need a few copies and yet want a slick "full color effect." If you find one of these clients . . . run. You won't like the results. If a client only wants to pay for 50 brochures what will they be willing to pay you? Just setting type for one of these faux brochures will take about two hours. That's $140 in our shop. At our rate a client would pay $2.80 per copy, plus designy paper and impression charges for 50 brochures. You won't find many people who want that service! Even with the amazing cost reducing power of the computer, publishers need to concentrate on long run jobs to maximize their income.

NEWSLETTERS

Desktop technology is largely responsible for the recent proliferation of newsletters. Large companies have used this format for sometime to communicate with their employees and build a sense of common purpose. A few large civic organizations have also used them to update their membership. Today, it seems that everyone from the local democratic club to Clides Burger Stand issues a newsletter.

how to use newsletters
Most newsletters fall in one of four categories: 1. Organizational Letters aimed at developing membership participation and a greater sense of participation, and funding support, 2. Corporate Personnel

Letters designed to communicate corporate goals and objectives, 3. Promotional Letters that deliver sales messages for specific products or services in the guise of news or information, 4. Informative Letters directed toward a paying readership.

If a newsletter works, it works because the reader believes he/she is being entertained and informed first and sold or proselytized second. Newsletters, at their best are the print media's version of the TV infomercials. They hold our attention, expand our knowledge, and lead us to the conclusions held by the sponsor. At they're worst newsletters are like a cheaply printed direct mailer, and like same, they go directly to the recycling bin.

print media infomercials

The most common flaw of any entrepreneur is the widely held belief that the public shares his concerns and wants to know all they can about his business. Therein lies the downfall of 70% of the newsletters we have examined. Each month we get a well designed and written letter from a printer. Problem is, it doesn't have a scrap of information that interests us. It talks about his staff, his new equipment, his new in-plant procedures. Those are his problems and triumphs. I want to know how fast he is going to turn my job around, how I can sell more printing to my customers, how I can cut costs and increase my profits. To succeed a good newsletter publisher must have the unique skill to set aside their personal interests and write from the reader's point of view.

content that performs

The ability to address relatively small populations is the stronge point of the newsletter format. Editions of 500 copies can be very cost effective. But, they are only effective when written in a highly focused style. The reader must be riveted to every word. Your audience should look forward to your next issue and save previous ones for their reference file. If you don't feel you can create that type of letter do yourself and your client a favor and pass on the job.

Fortunately, there is help for the blocked writer in the form of clip

"clip copy"

copy. Berry Publishing, 300 North State Street, Chicago, IL 6 0610, publishes a general interest newsletter called *PAGES* with articles that are particularly appropriate to publishers of corporate personnel letters. Subscriptions include the reproduction rights and it can even be delivered on-disk to avoid re-keying.

Professional writing assistance can usually be found in most localities. A favorite medium of the freelance writer has become the fax machine. Many highly experienced writers have found they can bill more hours at a lower rate if they never have to meet their clients face to face. They simply stay at home accepting and delivering writing assignments over the fax (or modem). If you have a direct modem you can even avoid keystroking the freelancer's work (be sure to check it for errors that can occur in transmission). Check the business services classified in your local paper and those in major cities. After all, it really doesn't matter where the writer is as long as he/she can deliver newsworthy articles of interest to your readers.

engaging writers   You might even strike a deal with a writer similar to the PAGES newsletter. Offer to purchase reproduction rights only for your publication, at a reduced rate. Indicate that you believe the article could be resold to any number of other publishers as long as they are not in direct competition with your client. Better yet, undertake the publication of your own version of a clip copy newsletter. Articles on teamwork, employee cooperation, salesmanship, goal-setting and attainment and negotiation are particularly appropriate for this type of venture.

house organ   Because of the cost-effective nature of the newsletter format, the possibilities for assignments are virtually limitless. Start at the top and work your way down. Many large corporations that already do an employee newsletter (sometimes referred to as a ***house organ***) might be pleased to send it out-of-house as a part of a staff cutting reorganization (so popular today). Armed with you ability to obtain filler copy at a good rate you could probably produce a nice monthly letter for less than they are paying to do it internally.

But this is just the tip of the iceberg. Look for small business that have developed a mailing list (one of the greatest assets a business can develop, by the way) and offer to tailor a letter to their clients and customers. Selling to those who have bought from you before is the most productive use of direct mail, prospecting for leeds usually isn't productive. Before approaching such a prospect, think carefully about the type of letter that will best serve their customers. For instance, a men's clothing store specializing in discount prices on quality suits will probably attract young executives concerned about corporate advancement. The obvious mix of articles would fall into the "Dress for Success" genera. But articles on negotiating, problem-employee management, motivation and high-tech advances will create a more rounded letter less apt to end up in the corporate trash.

Truly great newsletters, the ones that are saved for years, always contain useful tables and graphs of some sort. They can be comparisons of products by features and cost, such as, "How to Assess the Value of a Word Processing Program for Your IBM." You might consider devoting a single page to such a feature with your client's name displayed prominently at the top or bottom. In this way the reader could cut the page out and post it on his/her cubicle wall for easy reference. *features that ensure retention value*

Professional corporations such as large dental offices, chiropractic practices and law firms are also excellent prospects for newsletters. They can use the medium to discuss new technical advances or legislation of importance to their patients and clients while reminding their readers of their practice. *professional organizations*

Don't overlook the "not for profit" sector in your prospecting. Just because an organization is "non-profit" doesn't mean you can't profit by working with them. Many foundations, charities, and government agencies have a responsibility for "community out-reach" (a euphemism for letting people know what your doing). Newsletters are a great way to accomplish this with relatively small investment. In *not-for-profit organizations*

California, many state agencies are required to aggressively seek out minority business enterprises and women's business enterprises businesses (MBE and WBE) for a substantial portion of their contract work. Newsletters to the registered WBEs and MBEs serve to alert these companies to upcoming bid competitions.

minority and women's status   If you qualify as either a MBE or WBE in your state or locality, you should definitely register with the appropriate agencies and place yourself on all possible bid-lists. As a MBE/WBE you may receive an important percentage allowance on bids you submit. For instance, many government contracts are supposed to go to the lowest qualifying bidder. If you qualify on all other points you may still win even though your bid is 5% or even 10% higher than the lowest bidder. This special Minority/Womens preference is a technique used to encourage these groups to become involved in the public sector and discourage the "good old boys clique" that once received the bulk of public contract spending.

You would be amazed at the number of government and quasi-government agencies that are required to publish books, catalogs, newsletters and other documents. Much of the work is highly specialized and requires writing and research you may not be able to do alone. There are often public meetings prior to the opening of bidding on large contracts where the agency representatives explain the scope of the project to potential new bidders. These are excellent opportunities for small contractors to make important personal connections with agency purchasing officials and, perhaps more important, other contractors who may have the skills you lack. Well presented cooperative proposals from two or more contractors can often prevail.

Make no mistake, writing proposals for public contracts can be extremely frustrating. Great care must be exercised to comply with all aspects of the **Request for Proposal** (RFP). Some RFPs are the size of small books and require a law degree to interpret. The best avenue for most publishing MBE/WBEs is probably personal contact. The RFP usually lists one ore more individuals who are available to answer questions for bidders. Think of a question to ask, even if you don't have one. Be sincere, businesslike and persistent. If you don't win a bid, find out who did and why. It's public information and you're public. Ultimately everyone (bureaucrats included) works with people they like. Get to know the people in purchasing positions and gain their respect. You'll eventually get the jobs.

PRINT BROKERING

The largest single profit source for desktop publishers is the one most books on the subject ignore, printing sales. We have already spoken of copying and copy brokering (arranging for a third party to do the copying and thus making a markup). But, many of the projects you will compose will require professional printing service. Some clients will have favorite printers with whom they have worked for some time, but others will naturally turn to you for a printer recommendation. This is the perfect opportunity to say, "we'll handle your job from start to finish." Depending on the size and scope of the project you should be able to charge the client between 125% and 150% of your costs.

Some clients object to working with a printing broker because they believe there is no reason to pay an intermediary's mark-up. Reassure your client's that a good printing broker not only costs no more, they frequently save their clients valuable time and large sums of money.

It goes this way; no printer will turn down a job. If you walk into a print shop with a job that does not fit the shop's capabilities the person at the desk will take your boards and say, "thank you very much, we'll get back to you with a price next week." At that point one of two things will happen, either the shop will price the job forcing it to run on their equipment (very inefficient) or take it to a *job shop* (a printer specializing in working for other printers) that has the correct equipment. In the first case there is a good chance the job will not only be very expensive, but it will probably be botched. In the second

print brokers save clients money

case the printer himself becomes a print broker and makes a markup.

Because you are acting as both designer and print broker you can determine who will print the job before you finish your layouts. Therefore, you are able to tailor your mechanicals to the printer's pre-press and press capabilities. This alone, can save the client hundreds of dollars in mechanical and film costs. Some printers may have in-house Linotronic (or other) film capabilities and accept your jobs as pure data on disks. Knowing exactly how to prepare art for each printer is an important aspect of print brokering and the area in which the most time and money can be lost.

maintain current price lists

We spoke earlier of McGrew and other gang printers. They are listed in the resource section. Keep a current file of all their price lists. Generate a price list of your own for simple jobs. We have included a copy of ours for reference. Be sure your clients understand that this standardized pricing applies only to the simplest projects. Actually, you won't get many that fall into this category. No matter how hard a client tries, they can never conform to a gang printer's format. There are inevitably added charges.

develop printer data base

Although gang printers can be useful, they do have limitations. When faced with truly custom specifications local commercial printers can be less expensive. Develop a data base of printers grouped by equipment and capabilities. This will allow you to quickly and easily generate your own RFP form in programs like Microsoft *Word* or *FileMaker Pro* that have the ability to generate merge letters. The request for proposal (also called the request for quote) that we have included has served us well for many years.

We group our printers in the following data bases: 1. Full Service, Four to Six Color Sheetfed Printers 2. Web Printers, Four to Six Colors 3. Economy Printers, Two to Six Color, Sheetfed 4. Direct Mail Printers (usually lowest price and quality) 5. Book Printers (binding specialists) 6. Quality Instant Printers (usually a small local firm, may even be a franchise operator).

Begin by placing all the printers you can find in your data bases. *generating your RFQ*
Each time you receive a quote request from a client, simply enter it in
our form and generate merge mail RFQs from the appropriate data
base. To expedite service, fax your RFQs to the printers. Soon you will
narrow the field to one or two printers who's work is reliable and
who's prices will bare reasonable markup. We believe it is better to
build strong relationships with printers rather than demanding the
lowest price every time. Printers have the ability to shuffle jobs so
that better customers are served first. Much of your value as a print-
ing-broker is the ability to offer your customers outstanding service.
Moreover, a good printer will frequently cover your mistakes and enhance your relationship with your clients.

Some of your best profit opportunities in printing sales will come *off-shore printers*
from off-shore resources. In a way it is unfortunate that American
printers, like so many other American industries, have lost their competitive edge. This, however, is not a condition for which you can be
held responsible. The fact is, Japan, Korea, Hong Kong, Singapore,
Malaysia and Indonesia are all doing very high quality color printing
on the latest presses. With the exception of Japan, print buyers can
usually save one third the cost of comparable U.S. production, even
on moderate sized jobs. These savings include the cost of sea freight,
reasonable air courier costs (for transmitting art, film and proofs back
and forth) and a secondary broker.

Its unlikely you will want to become a primary overseas printing *off-shore film*
broker. It is a full time career in itself. Overseas printing brokers have *composition*
invested substantial time and resources developing their contacts,
working with prepress and printing resources and perfecting their estimating systems. These estimating systems alone are valuable and
complex assets because they must factor in freight, duty and constantly fluctuating currency exchange rates. We suggest you contact
several off-shore printing brokers in your area and ask what types of

jobs they do. Some brokers have minimums, others do not. Some brokers are pleased to handle just the film composition aspect of your printing. This can be a great asset on jobs with tight budgets and timetables. Well composed film with accurate proofs can be air shipped economically and printed quickly here. You will find many local printers who are more than happy to let you provide your own film and have no trouble dealing with separations done in Asia. Always work with brokers who quote in U.S. dollars and deliver to your location. Handling your own customs clearance is a colossal pain you don't need. Having a reliable Asian printing resource will mean you can offer your clients lower costs and that means you will be able to sell more printing.

PUBLISHING ON SPEC

For those with the true entrepreneurial spirit, there are greater rewards (and consequently, greater risks) in the business of speculative publishing (or publishing on spec). The term refers to any project assumed without firm guarantees of compensation and the process often requires substantial commitment of a publisher's time and resources with an uncertain payoff. For this reason the publisher is entitled to a far greater profit, should the project be successful. The publishing-on-spec business also provides the operator with a greater degree of artistic freedom. He is usually his own client with no nagging art director looking over his shoulder. This, however, can be a formidable problem to the novice who has become comfortable doing whatever the client wanted with no regard to their own tastes in page design.

DIRECTORIES

One of the most successful ventures for entrepreneurial publishers is the directory. They currently come in all shapes and sizes covering everything from small association memberships to national and international directories of businesses. Probably the most ubiquitous example of a directory is the Yellow Pages Phone Book. It's popularity stems from it's simple organization of businesses by type, thus end user need. This is the essence of all good directories. To be useful, they must serve the needs of a specific end user. Therefore, the questions to ask when developing a directory concept are:

1. What group of businesses appeal to a specific demographic? The Yellow Pages simply concentrate on businesses in a geographic area . But, we know people's shopping habits are effected by many more subtle discriminations. People want to shop where they feel comfortable, where the merchant speaks their language, shares their personal tastes, ethnic backgrounds and political convictions. This is the reason the Asian Yellow Pages, Hispanic Yellow Pages, Silver (senior) Yellow Pages, Gay Yellow Pages and many others have enjoyed remarkable success.

2. Is there a cost effective way to reach the businesses that appeal to this group? Because most directories depend on the sale of advertising for their income, you must be able to communicate effectively with your directory's participants and present a compelling advertising sales message. This is easiest when the businesses are already organized in some sort of association, like a chamber of commerce. You can simply ask to attend a meeting and make a presentation to the membership. It is slightly more difficult when the membership is wide-spread with no particular organization to recommend your project. This, however, can be an asset to the inventive publisher. With a little diligence and a well designed direct mail campaign you might form an association around the publication of your directory. If the association also has a beneficial civic and/or social agenda you might even consider incorporating as a non-profit organization, giving your project greater credibility. In any case you must find a way to sell advertising.

3. How will I distribute my directory. Is there an existing mailing list of my target market? It is difficult to imagine a group for which a direct mail list can not be concocted. Alternately, you might distribute to neighborhood gathering places such as community centers. Many directory publishers even rely on their advertisers to distribute a large portion of their books as "take-ones" on their counters or check out stands. This is only effective when their is little direct competition between advertisers. Still other publishers employ free stand-

ing magazine vending kiosks for distribution. Be sure to check local regulations before resorting to this technique.

Direct mail is by far the best distribution technique to impress *direct mail distribution* prospective advertisers and the best direct mail distribution is to a list of people who have specifically asked to receive your publication. It is easy to print thousands of copies of any ad and it is true that some novice advertisers will be impressed by the sheer volume of your press-run. But the savvy client who will return issue after issue wants to know how many books you placed in the hands of ready-to-buy prospects. For this reason, a prepublication direct mail effort to all potential recipients of your directory is useful. A two part, return reply card is a good vehicle to solicit interest. Simply describe your forth coming directory and ask them to complete the return portion of the card and mail it back for their free copy. You might even require the potential recipient to complete a brief questioner concerning their age, income and spending habits. Prospective advertisers would find this information quite valuable and your ad sales pitch will be strengthened.

If there is an existing magazine or newsletter directed to your tar- *developing your list* get market you can probably solicit a recipient list through an ad at a lower cost per thousand. Consider setting up an 800 number with an E-mail service bureau to receive your responses. This is a very cost effective and easy way to promote a variety of products and services. We have listed E-mail service operators in the resource section. Use your print ad to encourage prospects to;

> *"call for free information on how you can receive*
> *a valuable directory of _____."*

Both your ad and your out-going E-mail message can deliver a sales pitch that will heighten anticipation for your directory. At the end of your recorded message you will ask the caller to leave their name and address. You can access this data through any touch-tone telephone.

Besides exposing your project to potential recipients, the ad will develop interest among advertisers.

charging for your directory   Some publishers offering truly unique information have been successful in charging a modest fee for their directory, but this often reduces response and thus ad revenues. Still, if your data is valuable enough to your readers a distribution fee to cover printing and postage takes the pressure off ad sales and allows you to produce a higher quality publication. The following directories might warrant a paid distribution:

1. Directory of Discount Air Travel Resources
2. Directory of Low Cost Hotels in Major Cities
3. Directory of White Water Tours in Western U.S.
4. Directory of Little Known Grants and Scholarships
5. Directory of Services for the Handicapped or Elderly.

electronic directories   Although the majority of directories are "ink-on-paper", recent technical advances have made the publication of electronic directories popular and lucrative. Such publications can be up-dated daily or hourly in response to rapidly changing conditions. Techniques for publishing an electronic directory include:

fax directories   1. Fax-modem allows you to "broadcast" to a vast number of fax machines automatically. You simply compose your directory in your computer's hard disk, call up your data base of recipients (with their fax numbers), and command your fax-modem to merge-broadcast. Naturally this requires a fax-modem board, a fairly powerful computer and a dedicated phone line. But, if your data is time sensitive, your advertisers and /or your readers will be happy to pay the price. The publisher who does not wish to invest in the hardware to broadcast their own directory can avail themselves of MCI Mail, a service of the popular long distance company.

e-mail directories   2. E-mail is yet another technique to disseminate directory information quickly and efficiently. Some directory publishers prefer to use one of the popular communications networks to "publish" their directory. The publisher then collects a royalty for each time their directory is accessed by a user of the network. Networks include; Telenet (division of U.S. Sprint), Tymnet (division of McDonnel-Douglas).

The Directory of On-Line Data Bases is a vital tool for the electronic publisher. It is available from Cuadra Associates for $95 a year.

QUALITY-OF-LIFE BOOKS

Some form of the Quality-of-Life Book (QOLB) is published by virtually every Chamber of Commerce and/or municipality in the country. The purpose of the QOLB is usually twofold. First the Chamber of Commerce or other sponsoring organization uses it as a membership directory. They distribute it to the membership with the intention of promoting local business to business trade, thus earning the advertising rates. Second, and perhaps most important, it is used as an enticement to new businesses and individuals who wish to relocate to a town, county or region. In areas where travel and tourism are major contributors to the economy the QOLB may function as a tourist guide or an invitation to corporate meeting planners.

In fact, cities that depend heavily on conventions and tourism usually publish several books, each geared to the specific needs of a particular group. Although the basic book may focus on the community, it's resources, background, climate and economy, other publications may address convention facilities, hotel accommodations, family entertainment facilities or locations of historic and scenic interest.

The QOLB is very much like an expanded directory. Aside from a listing of the Chamber's members and paid advertisements of various sizes, the book usually contains: 1. lavish color photographs of the region's most picturesque locations, 2. articles describing the economy, educational facilities, natural resources, labor force, recreational facilities and natural wonders, 3. clever graphs and charts to support all vital statistics. 4. stylized maps to show easy access to major freight and transportation hubs.

Because the sponsoring body (usually a Chamber of Commerce) expects all it's members to participate in some way, your sales effort is greatly abetted. In fact, most member businesses have become accustomed to financial participation, thus you need only establish reasonable rates and contact the membership in a timely, organized manor. The Chamber will provide you with a letter of introduction and a list of the members you can solicit. It's a good idea to use copies of previous books to identify who placed the large full page ads. Theses are the contracts you will want to tie down first, the others will follow.

Most quality-of-life-books we have reviewed fell short of brilliant in their editorial, design and photographic content. This means there is a major opportunity for an aggressive, quality-minded publisher to not only capture new accounts, but to increase revenues on those accounts. Although many major cities with segmented quality-of-life-books may not wish to alter their well tested formats, smaller communities my be receptive to the following suggestions:

expanded QOL books   1. Expand the concept of the book to create a retailable volume that could be sold at local bookstores and newsstands. A large format perfect-bound or even a hard cover volume which featured articles on local history and the outstanding families of the region could be a strong seller as well as an effective QOLB. This would also increase advertising revenues through increased circulation.

calenders   2. Incorporate a monthly calendar with 12 scenic views of the community. This could be bound into the book or part of a shrink-wrapped package with the quality-of-life-book.

3. Communities with particularly scenic or historic merit may wish

to use the same photography generated for the book to create a series *postcards*
of postcards or greeting cards. These could be marketed locally as the
"official postcards" of the locality.

4. By donating a predetermined percent of the profits to a local *involve local charities*
charity and enlisting the charity's volunteers in the books sales you
not only gain a potent sales force, but capture valuable public support.

The quality-of-life-book can be an important vehicle to gain the
trust and confidence of influential members of a business community. When this project is completed professionally and on schedule the door will be opened to many other design and printing opportunities with the organizing body and it's members.

The QOLB is a more ambitious undertaking than we have dis- *preparation for initial*
cussed previously. It requires professional level research, writing, pho- *presentation*
tography design, print-production and management, and above all
salesmanship. Before approaching a prospective organization, begin
by reviewing issues from prior years. In this way you are able to formulate a sales strategy based on how you can improve the content
and presentation of their book. When you approach a town that has
no prior experience with QOLBs, accumulate books from similar localities with data to show how these book helped achieve specific
community goals. Develop a plan and proforma budget for the most
lavish book you believe the advertising base can support and carefully
structure a proposal to supply such a book based on the organization's ability to deliver the required number of dollars in advertising
revenue.

Bare in mind, that the sponsoring organization rarely experiences *ask sponsor*
any out-of-pocket expense in relation to such a publication. Your *to assist you*
costs and profit must be covered by ad revenues and any retail sales
you may generate. In fact, it is not unheard of for a Chamber of
Commerce to require a publisher to make a contribution of a percentage of their profits to the sponsoring organization. This is actual-

ly not unreasonable if the sponsor is willing to:

1. aggressively assist you in advertising sales,
2. devote office space and facilities to your organization,
3. solicit local photographer's work for use in return for photo credit.
4. convince local historical societies to give you free access to their archives and help you acquire the rights to the works of local historians.

the QOLB proposal process

Your initial proposal should describe your relationship with the sponsoring organization as a fruitful partnership, taking full advantage of all their resources and community contacts. A typical proposal for a quality-of-life book is shown in the appendix. Although you will be prepared to present a well developed proposal at your initial meeting, you must maintain flexibility in the early stages of negotiation. You are selling a package worth between $12,000.00 and $100,000 and your strict attentions to the sponsor's wishes and concepts is vital to a good working relationship. The sponsor's representative may even have some valid creative input that will substantially enhance the book and your portfolio.

Many volumes have been written on the subject of negotiation. Most begin by telling us to listen carefully to what the other party has to say. Nothing could be more valuable. The sponsor's representatives will give important clues to guide you in the formation of your proposal. Statements such as, "Business in this area has been soft this season," might indicate that you need a more modest vision of your project. While, "We need to attract more high-tech industry," sounds like an invitation to produce a lavish book. Use, the sponsor's representatives as your "inside" sales staff too. They usually know what type of project they can sell to their membership. If, after the initial discussion, you feel your proposal need further refinement, thank your prospect and make an appointment to present a formal proposal. There is nothing wrong in treating your first meeting as a fact-finding exercise. Your prospect will be flattered that you are not trying to sell them a cookie-cutter solution.

Most QOLBs are outside the production capabilities of single in-dividuals. Unless the QOLB you envision is an extremely simple pro-ject, you will want to surround yourself with ample staff or partners to impress the prospect with your ability to produce a complex work. Although the most obvious choice would be to hire writers, photog-raphers, designers, and a production manager, this may be the least economical strategy. All these skills are available as free-lance sub-contractors in most communities. Choose the rolls you wish to play and engage subcontractors to do the rest on a job-by-job basis. Many will be pleased to work for an agreed percent of the profits. This tech-nique will not only help you contain costs, but relieve you of the bur-den of producing monthly payroll reports.

developing a production team

Be sure to check with your attorney or your state department of human resources to be sure you comply with their definition of ***in-dependent contractor***. In some states an IC must perform a designat-ed percent of their function "off premises", or not in the primary contractor's facility. Other states may impose various requirements to qualify independent contractors. If your state audits your records and determines that you have actually been using your contractors as em-ployees they may force you to pay employee benefits and stiff fines.

independent contractors

Each subcontractor should receive a work-order defining the re-quirements of the job they will perform and the cost, including re-visions. The order should also state that copyright and use privileges will be held by the publisher (you) and that the publisher (you) has the right to revise and edit the work as necessary. A well planned time and action schedule should be incorporated in the client's pro-posal and the work order you use to the subcontractors. As we ex-plained in previous sections, the time and action schedule lets every-one (including the client) know what their responsibilities are and how long they will have to preform them. The schedule should make it clear that some penalty is applied for failure to meet the schedule.

structuring the work

In the case of a client, their project is delayed. In the case of a sub-contractor, it is customary to impose a daily penalty fee for every day past the deadline that their project remains incomplete. Naturally, when projects depend on the completion of other projects, failure to meet one deadline forces postponement of all deadlines. Thus it is wise to construct the schedule in a data base program that allows you to easily up-date it.

producing a mini QOLB   Many small communities find it difficult to justify large printings of elaborate books. Ten thousand copies would last 20 years for a small town. The the data would be miserably out-dated. Yet, they want a slick presentation when they approach important new developers or industries. These smaller communities can seldom support a quality-of-life publication through advertising revenue and probably shouldn't try.

Desktop publishers can provide a solution. Offer to compose a prototype book consisting of core information, history, climate, topography. Combine this with current data and photos and bind it as a comb or wire-o presentation. The color pages can be offset individually by a gang printer and the data pages can be printed in black and white or Xeroxed on a quality machine. You can provide as few or as many books as needed at any time. Keep the data on your system for easy up-dates and store the loose color pages in your office, ready for assembly.

Because you will probably produce less than 1000 books at any given time, you can hardly be expected to support such a project through the sale of advertising. Suggest that the sponsoring organization include a directory section of all their members. This might consist of a simple listing with name and address or a section containing quarter or half page ads that the members submit. The membership could be charged a nominal fee for participation or the organization might give the book and ad as a membership renewal bonus. You will charge the sponsoring organization:

1. an initial set-up fee to cover the core information section and printing,
2. a storage and retrieval fee,
3. an up-date fee,
4. a per book assembly fee each time they require more copies.

The organization will pay much more per book, but their presentation will always be current and they will avoid waste.

THE VALUE LETTER

One of the easiest and most profitable desktop projects is the *Pennysaver* or *Value Letter*. This document can take many forms from the traditional black, white and red tabloid on newsprint to the popular coupon packet or the Quality-Saver printed in a letter-size format on sulfite or bond and sometimes wrapped in a full color cover. The choice of your format depends largely on what already exist in your neighborhood and what local merchants might request. Naturally, if your advertisers consist of hardware and dime stores you will want to produce a more economical looking presentation than you might create for art galleries and antique stores.

why they work

The appeal of this media is based on three essential facts: 1. Everybody loves a bargain whether its on mouthwash or a Mercedes. 2. Most small retailers can't afford substantial advertising in major city newspapers. 3. Independent direct mail campaigns are also not cost effective for the small retailer.

franchised opportunities

In recent years several national marketing firms have recognized the potential for cooperative neighborhood advertising. Companies such as Advo Systems, The Ad Works and Val•Pak Direct Marketing Systems Inc. have established regional offices or sold franchises that make coupon or coop direct mail programs available to highly specific zipcodes. Most of these programs allow the merchant to buy as few or as many zipcodes as they wish. Some will even split zipcodes by carrier routes. Although these programs are attractively priced for the small advertiser, they are seldom effective because the vehicle they use is generally perceived by the recipient as junk-mail. The independent operator has the advantage of being able to tailor a publication to a specific neighborhood. With the inclusion of minimal amounts of folksy gossip or some interviews titled "Getting to Know Your Local Merchants" (also a great way to increase ad revenues) the independent publisher can produce a paper less likely to find it's way to the recycling bin. Features like community calendars or recipe exchanges can even get your value-letter taped to the refrigerator in half the homes you cover. Because of the lower costs of preparation and printing, even many small communities with weekly newspapers can benefit from value-letters that serve a small area of town, a subdivision or neighborhood.

use of coupons is essential   The primary appeal to the consumer is added value. Each advertiser should be strongly encouraged to print coupons that can be redeemed in their establishment for discounts, gifts with purchase, or services that carry a true perceived value. Image ad just don't work in this media and it is difficult for the merchant to track the results of a general sale promotion. If, on the other hand, 60 new customers walk through their door with a coupon from your publication in-hand the merchant will know they got their money's worth. Not only will they make a small profit from the initial discounted sale, but, more important, they have a face-to-face opportunity to win the favor of a new customer.

The production of the value-letter is not unlike any newsletter. What makes the publication unique is the fact that it is composed almost entirely of advertising. The publisher contemplating such a project should have their production strategies well under control and plan to spend the bulk of their time generating ad orders.

ad sales   A compelling sales presentation should include a graph or visual showing what the prospect would get in the major print media for the cost of a full page in your publication. Showing actual examples of the local newspaper next to your publication will further dramatize the point. Explain to the merchant that he is paying for unproductive circulation in the larger publication. Few people will seek out neighborhood businesses simply because they advertise in city-wide papers. The local merchant draws their customer base from 12 to 24 surrounding blocks and that is the territory you cover best. Also show examples of direct mail coop programs and explain how, unlike your media, they are perceived as "junk mail."

An interesting twist on the theme of value-letter is the *Free Church Bulletin.* Most churches publish a newsletter and / or Sunday Service Program. The preparation, printing and distribution of these documents places an added burden of the limited staff and budget of most churches. As a value-letter publisher, you could offer to handle all typesetting and printing in return for the church allowing you to include a tasteful advertising section in the back of the document. This is a truly win-win arrangement. The church gets a good looking, well printed program or bulletin and you get:

church bulletins

1. *added credibility;* A church newsletter program or bulletin is seldom perceived as junk mail. Most church bulletins contain a schedule of events which will lend retention value to your publication. Your readers will assume that their church is being supported by your advertisers, which is true in a sense.

2. *lower distribution costs;* You may wish to negotiate the cost of mailing any bulletin with the church. A 50/50 split of actual postage costs would seem reasonable. Of course the actual postage cost will be smaller if the church does the mailing with their non-profit organization bulk permit. You will also receive the benefit of the churches' mailing list and possibly the volunteer labor currently used to sort and prepare the documents for mailing or distribution at the religious service.

By enlisting the participation of several churches and synagogues in a moderate sized town, you could provide your advertisers with a substantial and well focused readership.

Other forms of distribution you might consider include:

distributing the value letter   1. Independent direct mail, This is the most expensive because you will not only have to pay bulk rate postage but you will also need to negotiate an on-going arrangement with a list broker or mail house to rent the names of your recipients. Remember, most list managers rent the names for one time use, unless a different prior agreement is reached. Violation of this agreement can lead to severe legal consequences. Many penny savers run "free subscription" campaigns because once a reader signs your subscription request you are no longer obligated to pay a list owner for that particular name. That name has become your name.

If your publication is directed to every household in a zip code you will be able to use an economical "occupant" list that your mailing house can provide. This list contains the properties in the zip code and the number of residences in each property, but no names. Most mailers substitute the word "Occupant" or "Our Friend at" If your publication is more sophisticated, you may have no choice but to use rented lists.

Another cost associated with the U.S. Mail is the preparation needed to qualify for the best bulk rate. The rules change from time to time but your local postmaster can keep you informed of the latest requirements. Basically your publication must be labeled and sorted by carrier route and delivered to the bulk mail division of the post office. This is usually in a warehouse far away from the actual post office. Unless you have access to a source of very inexpensive laborers and you are willing to supervise them, we strongly recommend you use the services of a mailing house. A good mailing house can process and apply labels, sort and bag mail and deliver it to the correct location for a very modest cost. Because of the volume of mail they handle they usually have a good relationship with the postmaster and can get favorable treatment of your mailings. Everyone has heard the horror stories of bulk mail sitting on platforms for weeks or, even worse, being trashed.

2. Because of the high cost of mail service many publishers opt to deliver their publication door to door via their own staff or with the use of a subcontractor. Some municipalities have anti-litter ordinances that impact this practice, so be sure you are in compliance before you dump bushels of paper on your neighbors steps. You may be required to go back and pick them up. Baring this possibility, and with the help of reliable low-cost delivery labor, most publishers favor this method for it's economy and the way it resembles traditional newspaper delivery.

independent distribution

3. Use your advertisers as a distribution network. A shopper who is already out and about town is the best prospect for your advertisers. Ask all your advertisers to display stacks of your publication near check-out stands. They will be more apt to comply if you provide inexpensive plastic or wire racks (see Seigal in Resources) to keep the display neat.

THE TOURIST GUIDE

No, there are no totally original ideas under the sun. Everything has been done in one form or another. But, the fun part of this business is the generation of ideas . . . one leads to another. For instance, if we combine the directory with the value letter and shove it into a small resort setting we come up with the tourist guide. Sure, the major cities all have hotel publications ranging from Que, a saddle stitched, vest-pocket sized magazine to the lush, full color, hard bound directories such as *City Guide*. But thousands of small sea-side and mountain resorts depend on tourists for their major source of income. And tourists need guidance. At best, most of them haven't been in the region for several months. They might not know about the Strawberry Festival or the Frog Jumping Contest. Worst of all, they might not know how to find your advertiser's establishment or about all the fabulous trinkets he has in stock. Virtually any town or region with 500 hotel rooms is a reasonable market for a tourist guide.

franchised tourist guides

Again, several national franchises have identified this potential market and even met with some success in selling local territories to individual publishers. They provide the franchisee with a format, into which the franchisee must pour their editorials on local interest, events and tourism, plus, of course, their advertising. The franchisor handles much of the production, printing and distribution, presumably at a lower cost than the individual franchisee might incur. Most of these publications look grim and fit the character of the individual communities they serve like a cheep suit. The publisher who creates a guide that truly reflects the town or region should have no difficulty in selling advertising, even in competition with a franchised guide.

sales strategies

One strategy is to glamorize the prospective location in a prototype edition and use it to close initial advertising sales contracts . Enlist the help of a local historical society to write features on "The Golden Age of Wherever." These features can be liberally illustrated with old photos of familiar street scenes contrasted with contemporary photos. Old maps of the area are another great fascination for locals and tourists alike. Above all, don't overlook the opportunity to create infomercials, profiles of local businesses and their proprietors.

On thorough investigation, almost every community is substantially more interesting than it seems to the casual observer. It is your responsibility as publisher of a tourist guide to find that "local interest" and present it in a highly readable format. Remember, people on vacation usually don't want exhaustive texts. Your publication should contain lots of pictures, lively captions and easy-to-read maps and calendars. If you are servicing an urban environment frequented by business people you may choose to publish a small format guide that can be carried in a vest pocket or purse. Larger formats may be more suitable for resorts or beaches. Color covers (at least on the outside) make your publication more appealing and ad sales easier. The amount of color you wish to run on the inside depends on the nature of your community and the amount of premium color advertising you can sell.

One of the primary advantages in publishing a tourist guide is the *distribution* ease with which it can be distributed. Although advertisers should be encouraged to make copies available at their locations, most of your distribution will be to hotels, motels and guest houses who will offer them in their guest rooms as a customer service. For this reason, it is important that your guide contain substantially more editorial and public service features than a value-letter. Well drawn maps highlighting locations of special interest and calendars of events are always welcomed features. An article on regional history can run issue after issue because most readers are new to the area. Articles profiling local businesses and tourist attractions can be recycled once every 12 to 18 months and up-dated as necessary. Thus, after the first 24 months of publication relatively little new editorial material is needed.

Another advantage is the ability to publish when you want. *publication schedule* Although the more popular and event oriented locations may demand a monthly guide, you may find it more relaxing and profitable to concentrate on smaller locations that can be serviced with one, two, three or four editions per year. Quarterly (or less) deadlines seem to be more flexible. No one will remember if your book is due out on the 10th of the month or the 20th. Some locations, mountain lakes for instance, lend themselves nicely to a biannual format. You can highlight skiing in the winter edition and fishing or water sports in the summer.

THE CITY MAGAZINE
You say you might become bored with the casual pace of the tour-

ist guide business, you say you long for the gut wrenching excitement of big time publishing, you say you have deep pockets and a longing to empty them? Well, welcome to the world of the city magazine. To be sure, the *city magazine* is a generic term applied to any slick, colorful, up-scale publication that concentrates on a geographic region.

New York Magazine   The first such publication was *New York* which began its life as a color supplement to the now defunked *Sunday Harold-Tribune*. It was one of the most sophisticated, urbane publications of its time. Its format was created by the renowned designer Milton Glaser and it was written by the brightest editorial talents. It was not uncommon to see the *Sunday Harold Tribune* discarded in a street receptacle sans *New York*, the reader more interested in the supplement than its somewhat stodgy wrapper. When the venerable *Harold Tribune* went south for the final time (or at least to Paris), *New York* lived on as a subscription and newsstand journal and spawned a legion of spin-offs and imitators. Although it is doubtful that any have equaled the commercial and journalistic success of the original, smart sums have been made (and lost) trying.

The most obvious problem faced by the city magazine publisher is the fact that few cities generate New York's breadth and depth of journalistic fodder. Like it or not, you just don't run out of material there. You can't say the same thing about Orange County California. Sure its nice, and so is the publication *Orange County*. It's just harder to maintain the same high standards month after month. Fortunately, advertisers don't necessarily pay for high standards, they pay for readership. And, most readers care intensely about what is happening in their back yards.

The city magazine is an adventure suited to the well financed risk-taker and a staff of marketing and production professionals, not for the faint of heart loner. Even in a rural community, success demands a high level of writing skills, salesmanship, promotion and cash-flow management. Both the cover and inside of your magazine should feature cutting edge design and photography.

The first step in developing a city magazine is a careful market *market analyisis* analysis. Your own home community may not be the best candidate for your enterprise, but one may exist near by. A major advantage of working near home is your ability to keep a finger on the pulse of your readership and advertisers. Selling to both is greatly facilitated if these are the same people you see everyday at the super market, church and golf club. Find a market with a sufficient concentration of retail businesses to support your publication, but with no competing magazine. The yellow pages is a good place to begin looking. If advertisers have bulked-out the yellow pages in a community they are likely pre-sold on the value of advertising and conceivably anxious to find a more dynamic media.

Establish a proforma (before the fact) profit and loss statement or business plan listing all your major expenses like this one:

PROFORMA PROFIT & LOSS STATEMENT
1. *recurring costs per issue*

distribution discount to retailers	5000.00
distribution to subscribers (postage)	6000.00
handling and freight to distribution point	500.00
printing	20000.00
stripping and make-ready	3000.00
typography	2800.00
photography	1200.00
film and processing	300.00
design and paste-up	10000.00
editorial	18000.00
ad sales commission	8400.00

2. *administrative costs*

management salaries and benefits	2400.00
support salaries and benefits	8000.00
marketing and events	6000.00
rent and occupancy	500.00
equipment depreciation and maintenance	1200.00
supplies	400.00
telephone and utilities	250.00
entertainment	300.00
sales promotion	500.00
taxes	6435.00
profit	10700.00
total monthly expenses	111885.00
Less newsstand & subscription sales	25000.00
Less subscription sales	45000.00
Net advertisers cost per publication	41895.00

Divided by 24 pages of advertising = 1746 per page gross advertising rate

Divide your annual expenses by twelve, then by the number of pages of advertising you plan to sell in each issue and you will arrive at your average page advertising rate. A modest size city magazine with a circulation of 40,000 per issue will run 90 pages (including front and back cover) and contain 24 pages of ads (including back cover). Therefore, an average page rate of about $1746 is within reason. This equates to a cost-per-thousand of slightly over $43. A little on the high side but not unreasonable for a trendy, up -scale publication in a market with no competition. Magazines in more competitive or larger markets should (and can) strive for a cost-per-thousand closer to $25.00 .

develop the rate card   However, establishing your entire rate card is more complex. You will want to create a rate matrix based on your average page rate that gives advertisers incentives for larger space ads repeated frequently. You will also charge a premium for placement on the back cover, the inside front cover and the inside back cover. Thus your rate card might look something like this one:

TYPICAL RATE CARD
Number Of Insertions in 12 Month Period Covers

	1X	3X	6X	9X	12X
back	$4333	4235	4138	4040	3943
inside front & back	4153	4060	3966	3873	3781
FOUR COLOR full page	2730	2667	2607	2545	2484
2/3 page	2196	2147	2098	2047	1999
1/2 page	1893	1850	1808	1765	1724
1/3 page	1043	1020	1499	1464	1429
TWO COLOR full page	2217	2168	2118	2067	2018
2/3 page	1679	1640	1603	1566	1527
1/2 page	1367	1336	1304	1275	1244
1/3 page	1043	1020	996	973	947
BLACK & WHITE full page	1866	1810	**1746**	1696	1642
2/3 page	1340	1299	1258	1219	1178
1/2 page	1067	1035	1002	971	938
1/3 page	741	720	696	675	651
1/6 page	411	400	386	374	363
CLASSIFIED 4 inch	363	351	341	329	320
3 inch	294	287	277	269	259
2 inch	201	195	189	183	177
1 inch	109	105	140	99	96

Note that the average page rate is in the center of the matrix in the black and white full page position.

Naturally these figures are highly idealized. No magazine ever ran this smoothly or profitably. If they did, everyone would be in the magazine business. The giant leaps of faith in our proforma come in the assumptions that; a) all our 30,000 subscriptions will be magically sold, b) all 10,000 newsstand copies will be eagerly snatched up, c) every inch of advertising will be sold at full rate. This never happens!

Once you have determined the economic basis of your magazine, develop a prototype issue with all the features, articles and even dummy ads. This prototype, or test issue, can will be useful in fine-tuning your editorial slant and as a sales tool for your advertisers. By this time your sales department should have a very specific list of target advertisers with a projection of the space each can be expected to order in each issue. Create actual ads for these clients or use pick-ups of similar ads they have run in other media. This will help your prospects visualize their business in the context of your publication. Convincing a prospect they are a "natural fit" for your media is often the most difficult aspect of closing the ad sale. "It just doesn't feel right for my business," is heard more often than the proverbial, "it costs too much." Demographic profiles and studies (which you must still produce) help less than visual conditioning to overcome the "feel" objection.

the prototype

Make several copies of your prototype issue. You may want to utilize a gang printer or an Asian printer (who still provides ink-on-paper press proofs) to accomplish this. Yes, this is an expensive process, but going to press with a full blown edition before you have readers, editorial styling, and advertisers in place can be disastrous. You will want to get the prototype read by as many people as possible. Ask for harsh critical comments on:

1. layout
2. photography

3. editorial content

4. editorial styling

5. features (Are they comprehensive? Should some be dropped and others added?)

6. overall service to the community, market.

Get this feedback from potential advertisers and community leaders. Where comments are positive, ask for the right to quote them in your promotions. Above all, do not show your magazine to a bunch of your friends who will feel compelled to say, "yes, very nice." You want constructive in-put and you will always be too close to your new baby to see its ugly birthmarks.

Your actual editions will probably be produced by one of the speciality magazine houses listed in the resource section. Magazine printing is a unique business requiring highly organized and automated systems and on-line bindery. Few commercial printers are capable of consistent performance under the time pressures of magazine publication.

production scheduling   When you are satisfied that you have as much feed-back as you and your staff can possibly absorb, when you have fine-tuned your editorial positions, when you have lined-up enough good writers, photographers, illustrators and designers to keep your editions lively, when you are convinced your rate card and demographic studies are adequate to sell enough advertising to cover your costs the real work begins. A magazine is, if nothing else, an exercise in scheduling. No flow-chart is too detailed for a project of this magnitude. We suggest you purchase, learn and use a computer generated system similar to **Critical Path** or *MacProject*. The key is to get copies of your flow-plan to everyone who is remotely involved with the magazine's production. The chart should illustrate how each individual's contribution relates to the whole (and the consequences for failure to deliver on time.) Your advertisers should be planning their promotions on your publication schedule. To disappoint them is suicidal.

editorial schedules   ***Suggestion:*** Many magazines theme each edition and publish a schedule of those editorial themes six to twelve months in advance. This helps advertisers coordinate with appropriate editorial content. For instance, fashion retailers might wish to appear in an edition largely devoted to the Paris Spring collections. Restaurants and ethnic speciality shops could capitalize on an issue devoted to a unique Russian neighborhood.

Some interesting alternates to the city magazine may fit the needs of your community (and your own skills) better than the full-blown publication described above. They include:

alternatives to city magazines

1. **A City Arts Publication** that concentrates on performance and/ or visual arts events in the community.

2. **A City Sports Magazine** that reports on high school, college and professional events plus the growing calendar of public participation events.

3. **A Neighborhood Tabloid** that focuses on one affluent region. This can easily become a social news-sheet for the entire city.

4. **A Community Year Book** that reviews the events of the city from January 1 to December 15 (so you have time to make Christmas delivery). This is a variation on the college year book, but for an entire town.

BOOK PUBLISHING

Hey, isn't that the kind of business that requires multi-million dollar investments, offices on Park Avenue, $300 lunches with publicity agents and international distribution? Yes, perhaps if you are planning to publish the next Norman Mailer or Alex Haley volume.

But, that's not what we had in mind. The small book publishing business can be very lucrative for all the opposite reasons. Today, taking a black and white manuscript to press is very inexpensive. There are many printers who can produce 1000 copies of your 208 page perfect bound book (from your laser printer original pages) for $2.75 to $3.25, depending on stock and size specifications. Properly designed, these books should look for all the world like those that retail for $15 to $30.

saddle stitched books   Saddle stitched books are even cheeper to produce but their market is limited almost entirely to mail order. The mail order book buyer is primarily concerned with the quality of information you are offering, not the presentation. Simply because saddle stitching looks cheeper and less substantial most bookstores won't carry these volumes bound this way. Many small publishers have found success with alternative *comb and wire-o* production techniques such as comb binding, wire-o binding or loose-*binding* leaf binding, all in combination with Xerox or short run offset duplication. These alternative techniques generally increase the cost of each unit but allow the publisher to make up books to order with little advance commitment to inventory.

Fine you say, but how do I unload this inventory regardless of size? *developing a*
The sale is in the concept! If you are driven to write and publish the *marketable concept*
next great American novel you may find yourself rowing up stream.
The market is flooded with good to great fiction vying for reviewer's
attention. But just write a good (or even mediocre) ***how-to*** volume
and the world will beat a path to your door.

As our economy evolves more and more Baby-Boomers will find
their work schedules and careers being down-sized (or eliminated al-
together). This massive reordering of the work force will lead to a
practice Alvin Toffler refers to in his book *The Third Wave* as "pro-
suming", a combination of self-production and consuming. The un-
employed computer programmer will find an opportunity to turn a
smart profit by temporarily accessing his IRA funds to buy a fixer-
upper second home, improve it and resell it. Trouble is, it needs a
new kitchen and bath. He has the time but not the skills. That's
where you come in. In fact, as the boom generation lurches toward
retirement in one form or another, many will find themselves with
more leisure time than money. Because we have all become so highly
specialized in our careers and lifestyles we will require a vast input of
"how-to" data in order to cope with this economic transition.
Everything from canning foods from our own garden to finding low-
cost accommodations in Nice will become grist for the information mill.

The ***how-to*** book will dominate the publishing market in the next
ten years and it may be one of the easiest books to write. Although a
reasonable command of the language is necessary, these volumes
don't require highly literate prose, philosophical insight or side split-
ting humor. The customer only wants to know how to accomplish a
task as quickly and easily as possible. The trick to writing a good ***how-
to*** is the same as the trick to selling one. Start with the end-user, the
market. Find any demographic, age, sex, geographic, occupational, ra-
cial, ethnic or religious group to whom a substantial direct response

media is focused (this is called identifying the market). Ask yourself, "what information will these people buy". Remember, the information must fulfill a basic human need. It should make them:

1. richer
2. healthier
3. more popular
4. sexier
5. more comfortable
6. more prestigious
7. more creative
8. more intelligent
9. more of any of the things we all want in life.

Its important to remember that very little of your book's content will be original. Very little in this world is. To be successful your book will be directed to a specific market and offer well researched information that may be available from other sources. What's important is that you assembled it and identified its importance to your target market. Let's look at some examples.

One of the most highly developed direct response (mail order) media is *Popular Mechanics Magazine*. Its classified pages are loaded with offers for instructions and plans to build a wide range of practical (and not so practical) projects. The sellers of these books, plans, pamphlets and brochures are generally quite successful, not because they provide revolutionary new information, but because they provide opportunities for their customers to display their creativity to family and neighbors. The editorial section of the same magazine may contain a similar plan, but the would-be inventor-craftsman prefers to send for the more obscure plan so he can adopt it as his own. The advertiser has thus made his customer more creative and intelligent.

The same principal is true of the vast number of advertisements for recipes in women's magazines and supermarket tabloids. Every community has a book store with cookbooks crammed with recipes from all corners of the earth. Women still prefer to invest a small amount in the hope they will discover something truly unique to boost their culinary reputation among friends and family.

One of the most popular and often abused topics for direct response book marketing is the "get rich quick" scheme. Although most rational, mature individuals realize there is no formula for overnight riches, there are enough people left who are daft or desperate enough to create a broad market for ill-conceived and badly written books on the subject. To be sure, there are many fine authors and publishers selling valuable business information through direct response.

It is far easier to write about topics on which you have direct personal knowledge. Research is time consuming and so is the process of transcription. For this reason we suggest you begin by exploring your own data banks. At first you may not believe you have much valuable information to offer others. Try listing subjects on which you might be considered expert, then list groups of people who might find this information useful. Don't stop at the obvious. How could you present the information you already have in a new context that would make it more vital.

adapt your knowledge to new markets

For instance, many people who enjoy wilderness hiking have learned to survive for several days from a modest backpack. Why not adapt this knowledge to a book on surviving natural disasters? You could discuss the correct provisions and tools to prepare for such an event, how to store supplies, dry foods, camp stoves, sleeping bags, tent, etc. You might even work with local emergency relief officials. Include their point of view and in turn get their endorsement for your project.

On the other end of the spectrum is the pure research book which may consist of nothing but a data base of resources. The reference section of major city libraries is an incredible source for the compilation of a data bases. It contains directories on practically every subject imaginable. As always, begin by identifying the market. Find a direct response media that's chock-full of book or information offerings. Don't worry about competition. The media with no similar advertising is sure to be the wrong place for you to advertise. Ask yourself, "what resources do these people need." Then find it in your nearest city library and compile it on a note book size computer. Most libraries don't allow you to remove large reference volumes from the premises. In some cases you might have to use the library's data to solicit additional information. Although time consuming, this is easy to do with a standard merge letter generated in MicroSoft *Word* and .

creating and selling data bases

Some examples of useful data bases might include:

1. A list of organizations that sponsor an annual meeting of 1000 or more participants.

primary resource: Gales Directory of Organizations This may require additional research. Send a letter to all the larger organizations. Ask how you might become a member. This will more likely assure a response. Then ask if they are planning a large meeting, where it will be, how many members are expected and who is coordinating the function.

market it to: event planners

market it through: Special Events Magazine

headline of ad: Capture You're Share of the Profitable Meeting Trade with our directory of organizations.

m*arket it to:* would-be event planners market it through: *Success Magazine, Entrepreneur Magazine, Successful Opportunities Magazine,* etc.

headline of ad: Earn Up To $150,000 Per Year as a Meeting/Events Planner! (requires additional text on meeting and event planning process).

2. A list of low cost wholesale resources for gifts and novelties.

primary resource: Hong Kong Trade Development Council Directories (these massive volumes are categorized by merchandise type and available in business libraries or direct from the Council).

market it to: would-be direct mail operators market it through: *Success Magazine, Entrepreneur Magazine, Successful Opportunities Magazine, National Enquirer,*

headline of ad: Make $150,000 a Year Selling Gifts & Novelties with Incredible Mark-Up Potential! (give specific examples). *You have probably seen this ad for years in several magazines, and even on TV.*

market it to: small gift store owners market it through: direct mail to a list of those attending regional gift trade shows, available from the show promoter headline of ad: Dramatically Increase Your Profits, Deal Direct With Asian Manufacturers, It's Easy!

3. A list of companies or organizations that publish newsletters by geographic region.

primary resource: Oxbridge Publishing, *Directory of Newsletters*

market it to: desktop publishers and small to midsized printers

market it through: *Desktop Magazine, Publish Magazine, Aldus Magazine*

headline of ad: Sell Your Printing & Publishing Services to the Lucrative Newsletter Market.

MARKETING YOUR BOOK

What is the best way to market a new book? The answer to this question is, *every way possible.* The key to entrepreneurship in the 90's is the multiple channel approach. Rather than concentrating on a single monolithic strategy the new entrepreneur is exploring every possible income source, every marketing channel, every sales lead. Yes, some marketing techniques will be more productive than others. By identifying the more productive techniques and concentrating on them you will maximize your sales. Our point, however; is don't guess what will work and what won't, test every possible marketing avenue.

The single most important event in the marketing of a book must take place before the pen ever hits the paper. A successful self-publisher (or any publisher, for that matter) must decide if there is a substantial market for the book they envision. This market must not only be large enough to warrant the publisher's efforts, but it must be relatively well organized and easy to reach. If we find there are print and broadcast media directed to our target market and trade shows and expositions with a similar appeal we have discovered an organized market. One of the most common reasons for publishing failure is the pension of authors to create books on such obscure subjects they are impossible to market. You may be the world's foremost authority on gorilla behavior but unless you can relate your knowledge to a mass market benefit you had better write a book on baking chocolate chip cookies.

marketing "local interest books"   This is not to say that every book published must be a block-buster best-seller. On the contrary, desk-top technology has made the publication of limited market books such as *local histories* commercially viable. It is important, however, to do some preliminary market research if you believe your book's appeal will be confined to one locality or isolated interest group. As we discussed in the section on periodicals, a two part *return-reply* postcard or an ad in an appropriate periodical could be used to solicit interest in your book.

For instance, suppose you were considering the publication of a children's book on the history of Monmouth County New Jersey. You might take a small ad in the *Asbury Park Press* or the *Freehold Transcript* asking for the submission of material on prominent family histories. The ad might also ask for editorial suggestions from school teachers and librarians. *See the sample ad in the appendix.*

This simple ad or direct mail card will:
   a. guide your editorial focus,
   b. create a sense of community involvement,
   c. pique interest in your up-coming publication,

d. help pre-sell the edition.

Not a bad investment! Strangely enough, the most productive feed-back you might get from such an ad or mailing is 0, no response (or a very weak one). This would tell you one of two things; either the list or media you used was the wrong one to reach your market, or more likely, there was no interest in your project. At this point, the determined publisher with money to loose will test other media. The more prudent publisher will test other projects. The fool will forge ahead regardless of the test results.

Many publishing beginners overlook or severely underestimate the value of unpaid publicity. Some experienced publishers sell more books through unpaid publicity than through paid advertising. This is possible because; 1. the public perceives book reviews and press coverage as an unbiased, third-party endorsement and 2. there is virtually no limit to the amount of publicity you can obtain when you don't have to pay the high costs of ad production and lineage. Notice we didn't say anything about "free publicity." There is very little of that around. Publicity costs work, and sometimes a little cash to prepare your materials for the media. Aggressive publishers have even been known to spring for lunch for a particularly influential reviewer or talk show host. But that's the exception.

developing a publicity campaign

All over the world thousands of publications are starving for newsworthy material to fill their editorial columns. Thousands of talk show producers are disparately looking for interesting guests to fill air-time. Millions of meeting planners are looking for speakers to present to their assembled throngs. By filling any or all of these needs you can perform a far more useful service than picking up a lunch tab and you'll serve your own purpose as well.

The first and most obvious source of publicity for the publisher is the book review. No, you probably won't be reviewed by *The New York Times* on your first volume out, but there are many fine publica-

getting a book reviewed

tions who's editorial opinion carries equal weight with their readers. They are listed in *Literary Market Place*, an indispensable volume found in most city libraries. It's also your one-stop source for radio and television interviewers who frequently host book authors. Use a notebook computer or file cards to create a data base of print and broadcast media that might be interested in your book. Naturally, you will concentrate on media that serves your targeted market. Forget *Field & Stream* if you're selling a book on make-up tips.

press kits   Once you have your data base you can begin to create publicity packages or press kits. Because of the lead time requirements of most media, this should be done 12 to 16 weeks before your book comes off the press. You don't want to sit with an inventory of unsold books any longer than necessary. Your press kit should consist of a professionally prepared two pocket folder with your publishing company's name foil stamped on the front. Use a conservative dark color like hunter green or burgundy. This will command more attention than white without looking garish. Quality press kits are available from Graphic City, Inc. 8648 Dakota Drive, Gaithersburg, MD 20877, (800) 327-1070, for as little as 83¢ each for 3000 or in quantities as low as 50 (for 3.95 each). Other press kit sources are listed in the resource section.

press kit photos   The kit should contain a photo of the author and a short biography (one page or less). If possible, a photo of a mocked-up book can ad credibility to the package. This is not difficult to accomplish. Simply produce the cover design on your computer, out-put it to a Cannon LaserColor® printer (or other high quality color out-put) and spray mount it to an existing book of equal size. Be sure all photos are sharp, clear and contain little or no background distractions. Never use photos smaller than 8" x 10" or snapshots that look like they record a family outing. Bad photos scream "amateur" to media types so if you aren't a proficient photographer, spend a little more money and get your photos done right. Many towns have quick portrait studios that can shoot you and your creation for under $30.00.

The core of the press kit is the *news release*. It should consist of at *the news release* least one page (but probably more) of copy summarizing the major topics of your book and telling the prospective reviewer why his readers/viewers will be interested. Like all great ad copy, it must be written from the reader's point of view. Remember, the reviewer/ producer/ host who will read your copy is constantly under pressure to generate more popular stories or programs that will increase his publication's/station's circulation/audience. It is up to you to convince him that his readers/audience has a burning desire to know more about your subject and that you are the one able to enlighten them. Use articles from the popular press or refer to other broadcasters who have recently featured similar stories to reinforce the fact that the public is truly interested in your speciality.

Above all, your news release must emphasize the news-worthiness of your book. One more book on public speaking will never make the front pages. But, suppose the author developed a new technique to help people overcome their fear of public speaking through hypnosis? This might get someone's attention. The spark that ignites the interest of the media may be a relatively small feature of your book. If you believe you have created a work of merit and value you should be prepared to use almost any reasonable "angle" to bring it to the public's attention. On special occasions this even inspires minor rewrites to include material known to be favored by certain reviewers.

One sure way to to get the media's attention is through the in- *endorcements* clusion of a page or two of powerful endorsements from well known authorities in your field, (or well known anybody for that matter). Reviewers and producers are only human and thus often distrust their own judgment. If you can reinforce their interest in your book by showing that prominent authorities are also interested you will definitely have a leg up on the competition. If you believe it might be difficult to get "big name" endorsement for your modest little creation we had better mention the *Law Of Synergistic Promotion.*

"Big names", "stars", "celebrities", what ever you want to call them have become what they are for two reasons; 1. they have done something well (sing, dance, write, produce, research, design, etc.,) 2. they have worked hard to bring their achievements to the public's attention. The world is full of unknown geniuses, people who believe they should be rewarded for simply doing a good job. WRONG! You have to work at public recognition. Thus the "big name" understands that if you sell 200,000 books and run an ad seen by 500,000 readers with his endorsement prominently displayed on both, he will have the opportunity to remind 700,000 people that he is a "big name." Your modest little creation and the promotion you give it will do as much for him as he will do for it.

This is the *Law of Synergistic Promotion* and this is why you should bundle advanced (unbound) copies of your manuscript the minute you are finished with the final proofing process and send them to as many important authorities in your field as you can locate. Use the *Who's Who* volumes in the reference section of your library to locate names of potential contributors, but don't stop there. If you have written a general interest book, send it to local and state politicians, celebrities, anyone who's name is well known in a positive context. No, not everyone will respond. Some will even respond negatively, but if you have produced a quality product you will receive enough positive endorsement to make your job of promotion much easier.

exchange articles for "source boxes"

Another technique that adds power to your press kit is an offer to write an article for the publication in return for a *source box* . This is a small box at the end of your article that lists your qualifications on the subject, the books you have written and your publisher's name and address (one more example of why you must create a name for your publishing company that doesn't include your personal name). Many publications will resist this blatantly commercial request, others will oblige as long as you don't turn the source box into a direct mail ad, still others will let you do about anything you want in exchange for the filler copy they so desperately need. Accept all offers, (short of those that refuse to even give you credit for the article.) Whether or not it leads to direct book sales, every positive exposure will bolster your name recognition. When the reader of your magazine article recognizes your name in the bookstore (or direct response ad) he will already have accepted you as an authority of some stature, thus making his purchase far more likely After all, you are going to excerpt the article from your already completed book.

Although composing your articles should not require much effort or additional research, you should try to give your material a fresh slant and write in a style consistent with the publication's other articles. Don't merely copy pages from your book. Above all, don't mislead an editor with the promise of an "exclusive" when you are giving the same rehashed material to three other publications. This is a tightly knit industry and cheaters are quickly exposed.

Always include a **bounce back card** in your press kit. This is a simple and easy way for editors and reviewers to request an advanced copy of your book if they intend to review or mention it to their readers. A simple, effective card is 4.25" x 6" with your name and address (or that of your mailing house) on the front with the correct "return postage guaranteed" form. You may go to a your local post office, pay a modest fee and apply for your own return postage permit. But its easier to use the services of a local mailing house who will usually allow you to use their permit. If you are contracting for other mailing services, such as bulk mail processing, the mail house is the least bothersome way to go.

bounce-back card

The back of the card should contain space for the editor's or reviewer's name, publication, address, phone number and fax number. You may want to provide this information in the form of a second mailing label you can generate from your data base. Everything you do to make it easier for the reviewer to select your book makes it more likely you will get the publicity you want. If you do provide a label for the card, be sure to ask the recipient to make any appropriate corrections. Current, accurate media contacts are the life blood of the PR business. Some PR practitioners also ask the perspective reviewer questions about their market size and penetration or their demographic profile. Frankly, you should already have this information if you are going to the trouble and expense of contacting publications.

Finally, if your book is a coffee table edition or richly illustrated you may wish to enclose a composite sheet showing one or more of your most elaborate spreads and/or your cover in full color. This is optional and should only be considered for books with a strong visual appeal.

coop promotions   Twice a year the Publishers Marketing Association, 2401 Pacific Coast Highway, Suite 206, Hermosa Beach, CA 90254, mails a catalog of 38 book titles to 2500 major newspapers. The recipients are encouraged to request review copies with an enclosed bounce back card. Many general interest publishers find this an effective tool. You may contact the association for more details at (310) 278-2213.

public appearances   You now have a strong publicity package that should knock the socks off your targeted print media moguls. Unfortunately, that's just one third the picture. The other two thirds of your PR campaign should target broadcast media and associations. More books are sold in America as a result of broadcast and personal appearances than through any other form of promotion.

*"You mean I have to meet the public . . .
perhaps even speak to them?"*

Yup, you've got it, and if your aren't good at it, get good. It's the single most powerful tool at your disposal. Haven't you ever pondered why even mega-stars like the late Joan Crawford appeared in relatively small shops to autograph their books? The answer is simple, personal appearances generate sales. You may never match the book selling success of Joan Crawford and Elizabeth Taylor, but that's no reason to shun their well proven sales techniques. If you don't currently feel prepared to undertake speaking engagements you might want to take a course on the subject in a local community collage or join *Toastmasters*, a national organization that helps prepare people for public speaking. It's a wonderful discipline that opens many doors for the average person. Just gaining the ability to speak to a room full of people and effectively sell your book is well worth the small investment in training.

Using *Gale's Directory of Associations* (available in most library reference departments) compile a data base of associations that might be interested in your services as a speaker. You'll be amazed at the number of potentials within easy driving distance of your home. Start with those. Send them a letter of introduction, a press kit which might include a list of other successful speaking engagements you have completed and a proposal outlining the conditions under which you will appear. Ask them to indicate a desirable date and other alternate dates, sign the proposal and return it to you at their earliest convenience.

targeting associations

If you are a famous, and accomplished speaker you can ask for the moon, i.e. a big fee plus the sale of your book in the back of the room. Normally the sponsoring organization will man the sales table and receive a 30% commission on book sales, but this is negotiable. If you are less accomplished or notorious you may want a more modest fee or settle for a book sales arrangement. Some organizations will invite you to speak and provide neither fee or sales arrangement. Don't be too hasty to turn down this invitation if the organization can provide a substantial audience that would logically be interested in your book. Nothing will prevent you from mentioning your book (and the fact that it is available in better stores everywhere) in the course of your presentation. And suppose it isn't available everywhere? Perhaps your appearance is just what is needed to create a ground swell of demand in the local shops. Direct sales or not, an organization that can deliver a large room full of potential buyers is worth a speaking engagement.

Once you have exhausted the organizations within driving distance of your home you may want to consider a speaking tour, but not before you have tried one other technique. Speaking tours can be expensive, you must book larger crowds and sell more books to off-set the added cost of travel and hotel accommodations. Broadcast media can deliver those larger audiences in one neat stop, sometimes without leaving home.

targeting broadcast media   Make one more trek back to the reference section of your library and find Bacon's Radio and Television Directory. If you expect to be doing a lot of this work you might invest $250 for your own copy from Bacon Information Services, 332 South Michigan Avenue, Chicago, IL 60604, phone (312) 922-2400. This terrific resource lists virtually every radio and television station in the country with a complete profile of their programming policy and features. Also listed are names and addresses of programming directors and major editorial executives, so your press kit will get to the right person more quickly.

By now you are an old pro at concocting a press kit to whet the appetite of editors and producers. If you have previous on-air interview experience send a tape, video or audio, of that interview to demonstrate your on-air skills. If this is your first experience in broadcast, be sure to ask for a tape of your segment so you can dupe it for future press kits. There are several companies that specialize in low cost tape duplication. A 10 minute audio tape can cost as little as $.65 and a 15 minute video tape will run about $ 4.50 in lots of 200. Resource: Dove Enterprises, 907 Portage Trail, Cuyahoga Falls, OH 44221-9983, Phone 800-233-DOVE or 216-928-9160 National Cassette Services, Inc. 613 North Commerce Avenue, Front Royal, VI 22630, Phone 800-541-0551 or 703- 635-4181

Don't over look your local media. If you live in a secondary market (other than a major city) the fact that you wrote a book will probably be enough to get you before the cameras.

You might even consider asking a local radio or TV station personality to help you with your on-air presence. Many of the talented people at small stations are poorly paid and welcome the income from consulting on their off days. In this way, even the totally in experienced publisher can prepare an audition tape. Plan to spend an entire day with your chosen consultant and schedule an hour in a local video recording studio for the end of that day. If there are no studios in your town contact one of those ubiquitous wedding video specialist. Have them tape a mock interview with you and your consultant.

preparing for a successful media appearance

Careful preparation is the key to a successful audition tape. If you have written a book on wood-working and have a well equipped shop, you may want to give a location interview. If your book deals with theoretical matters a studio or living room may be the best location. Always prepare a list of questions you want the host to ask, but never rehearse the exact questions and answers. Prospective producers and hosts look for guests that appear spontaneous and field difficult questions comfortably.

develop an audition tape

This may seem like a lot of effort to get a few broadcast interviews but virtually every successful publisher exploits this technique. They know they could never afford to buy the equivalent amount of paid commercial exposure available virtually free from news hungry broadcasters. Especially when you consider you might not even have to get dressed to attend some of your interviews. Many radio talk show hosts are so desperate for interesting guests that they will interview you over the phone. This format is particularly popular with call-in shows where the public is also encouraged to participate with live questions and comments.

By the way, do you think the successful publisher mails his press kits to his target editors and producers, then sits back and waits for a response. Think again. Although the targeted editors and producers have a constant need for new material, they are also besieged by hundreds of requests for media attention. Although most of these requests are less interesting and more self-serving than yours "the squeaky hinge gets the oil." You must develop a methodical program of follow-up calls. Be a pest and be prepared to restate all the audience (reader) benefits you outlined in your press-kit. If they can't give you an answer at that time, ask politely if you can call back in a few days. Above all, leave the impression that you have a burning news story that the public deserves to know about. It is often easier to make these important calls if you introduce yourself as someone other than the author or publisher. You might call yourself George, the manager of press relations. This will allow you to be more enthusiastic about the project without seeming grossly immodest.

use professional PR sources　　Finally, the serious publisher who feels his time would be better spent developing new products can assign many of the routine public relations functions to a contractor such as Bacon Information Services (mentioned earlier). Bacon will use your press release and photos to create a press kit to your specifications. They will generate a mailing list from their massive databank that will suit your book's interest profile. They will assemble and mail everything, saving you hours of drudgery. You probably couldn't do it cheeper if you paid yourself only minimum wage. Moreover, Bacon can fax your press release to it's huge data base in less than a day and arrange for European delivery of releases. Using the resources of a contractor like Bacon could vastly accelerate a publicity campaign.

BOOK SALES-*CONVENTIONAL & NOT SO*

Although the small independent publisher will almost always be better served by unconventional distribution techniques such as direct response and their own distributor network (more about these later), you should not totally dismiss the value of the more traditional distribution channels. Although nearly 50% of the volume done in America's bookstores is controlled by national chains there are still opportunities for the independent press in retail if you have created a product with wide general appeal.

When considering retail, your first decision is whether to deal *distributors* through a distributor or deal direct. Because the retailer will expect a 40% discount on the retail price of books purchased and the distributor will expect an additional 10 to 15% your choice might seem obvious. Actually, if your book has only regional appeal and you wish to target the smaller non-chain stores in your area you would be wise to forgo the services of the distributor. However, it is extremely difficult for a small publisher to sell to chains, or for that matter to sell outside of their geographic region, without the assistance of an established distributor. Buyers are reluctant to write small orders to unknown vendors (publishers) who may or may not be around when its time to return unsold books or reorder run-away best sellers. Distributors provide the assurance of a predictable flow of goods and accountability over the long haul.

Distributors also provide an important margin of safety for the small publisher. Strange as it may seem, there are retailers who have no compunction about late payment (or even non-payment) of invoices to vendors they don't consider crucial to their business. This can be particularly treacherous for small publishers with only one or two titles on the retailer's shelves, especially if title sales are down-trending. Distributors who may provide 10% of the retailers stock will have far more leverage in the collection department.

invoice collection and distributors

Literary Marketplace, published by R.R. Bowker and available in the reference section of major libraries lists most book distributors. Choose those who specialize in your subject or geographic area and send them a press kit similar to the kit you prepared to generate publicity. However, the distributor kit should stress:

1. any previous retail experience your book may have (i.e. sold 60 copies in 5 days at Clarks Book Emporium, Dayton, Ohio)
2. schedule of up-coming appearances you have planned to promote sales.
3. schedule of up-coming ads to promote sales.
4. any other factors which might lead to a period of rapid sales or high demand (i.e. book on backyard barbecue . . . just in time for Summer cookouts)

Follow-up your mailing in about a week with a personal call. If the buyer doesn't feel he can represent your book ask for a referral to another distributor. A distributor's reluctance to handle a specific book often has less to do with the book's quality than it's similarity to one already carried by the distributor. Distributors seldom want to compete with their own titles.

R.R. Bowker publishes yet another volume of vital importance to small presses, the *American Library Directory*. It lists virtually all libraries and acquisition librarians in the United States and Canada. This can be one of your single largest markets. Librarians respond to public demand, thus all the techniques we have discussed to generate this demand should also be focused on the librarian. Naturally, you *sales to libraries* would like every man, woman, and child to purchase a copy of your book. But, if they don't you would like them to ask their local librarian to purchase it. Oddly enough, having library access to a book frequently stimulates direct and retail sales, particularly if the book is highly detailed and not very expensive. People will purchase books to which they refer frequently, especially if they retail for under $50.

Librarians also respond to positive reviews in *BOOKLIST* (they only print positive reviews), a publication of the American Library Association, 50 Huron Street, Chicago, IL 60611. Be sure the Adult Book Editor is high on your list when you are sending out review copies. There are also distributors who primarily service libraries. One of the best is Quality Books, 918 Sherwood Drive, Lake Bluff, IL 60044-2204, phone (312) 295-2010. Others can be found in the *American Book Trade Directory*.

EXPANDED RETAIL

Although most publishers consider bookstores their primary retail *alternative retail out-lets* outlet, the small desktop publisher should consider alternate retail establishments. How-to books sell particularly well in speciality stores dedicated to the book's primary interest. If you have written a cookbook, visit local housewares speciality retailers. Ask the buyer to carry your book, but more important, ask what distributors service their market. Contact these distributors and show them how they can round out their line and provide added service by carrying your book. Speciality retailers such as nurseries and home improvement centers like authoritative books that relate to their merchandise. Although books may not provide as great a mark-up as other items, they provide important service to their customers, enhance the customer's interest in other product lines and ultimately lead to greater sales.

Publishers are often pleasantly surprised that speciality retailers de- *aging practices* mand smaller discounts than book stores and almost never return unsold books (a common bookstore practice.) Another distinct advantage of the speciality retailer is their ignorance of the aging practice of many large publishers. In order to force more product through the "pipeline" many large publishers condemn their releases to a premature death sentences. Books are ready for the mark-down tables in as little as four to six months after publication. Large publishers want a quick burst of sales and a slow dwindling period thereafter. Then they are on to the next "blockbuster." Small publishers who frequently release their own work want quite the opposite. It is not uncommon for a small publisher to enjoy 10 years of steady sales from one title. Of course the book will undergo many printings and several revisions during that time. But, the initial investment of effort and research will pay long-term dividends. Because speciality retailers are not tied to the publishing establishment, as are most book-sellers, they won't treat your book like soiled goods while it's contents are still fresh and relevant.

dumps   Although you may find retailers from lumber yards to body-oil boutiques eager to carry your books, not many will be good at presenting them. If you depend on a minimum wage clerk to accommodate your volume in his display of other goods your book could languish in the stockroom. When selling to retailers other than bookstores, it's a good idea to offer *dumps*. These are display units that come in a number of shapes and sizes. They are usually made of die-cut corrugated board, although they can also be wire or plastic. Some publishers provide floor-standing dumps that can be placed near front doors and in other high traffic areas. Large publishers frequently use lavish four color printing to draw attention to their dumps. The small press will be well served by simple counter-top dumps that can be printed in one or two colors and project the major user-benefits of the book they contain. Corrugated dumps are available from ABEL express, 230 East Main Street, Carnegie, PA 15106, phone (412) 279-0672, or Alpak Manufacturing, 185 Route 17, Mahwah, NJ 07430, phone (201) 529-4444.

We have even heard that some desperate small publishers were visiting the trash compactors behind large book chains' outlets. Frequently publishers ship books in dumps which are discarded in unused condition. With the applique of some artful laser printer output these dumps can be recycled to serve the small publisher's needs.

CREATE A DISTRIBUTOR NETWORK

As you become more familiar with the book publishing business you will discover you are not alone. Dozens, perhaps hundreds of other small publishers are operating in your area(s) of interest. The successful ones have chosen to concentrate on one or two narrow topics. Many publishers have written books similar to yours, others have written books dealing with the same topic but with a totally different focus. It is likely that the well informed reader will want the opportunity to purchase all the important books on your subject, regardless of minor overlaps in data. You will find other publishers who have written on topics closely related to your area of interest. For instance, the work of a publisher dealing primarily with "public speaking" "publicity for small businesses" or "how to handle media interviews" should be of great interest to an individual concerned with book publishing.

The astute publisher also realizes his business is divided in three distinct sectors; production, marketing and fulfillment. To be successful he must develop systems to accommodate all three tasks. Once accomplished, he may use these systems to produce, market and fulfill his own product or that of others. Because the systems are in place the added (or incremental) cost of processing additional product is minimal. Thus the more product = the more profit. Stated another way; never try to market just one book. The second, third and fourth book go along for the ride almost free and they vastly improve your profit performance. So what if they aren't your books, as long as they are quality books you feel comfortable endorsing? Make arrangements with other publishers large and small to promote their books in your advertising, direct mail and fulfillment brochures (sent out with your fulfillment packages). Suggest that these publishers also sell

the publishier's work is divided into three categories

maximize marketing efforts with multiple titles

113

your book and offer them a similar discount (usually about 40%). In this way you will create a symbiotic network of publishers, each of whom will look more authoritative because of their breadth of offerings.

backlisting   No, you won't get rich selling other's publishers books at 40% and it would be unwise to spend the effort or money to promote other's books exclusively. But, whenever you consider printing a package stuffer, making a presentation to a group, giving an interview, developing a press kit or any other promotional effort you should consider *backlisting* other publisher's work. *Backlist* is a publishing term that usually refers to the older (less current) items on a publisher's list. We use it here to refer to books of secondary interest to your sales effort. You might go as far as to ask other publisher's to discount their works deeply enough to allow you to wholesale them. Conversely you might make the same offer to other publishers. The advantage you will gain is increased press run, thus lower incremental cost. For instance, if you print 5000 copies of your book your unit cost may be $3.00 each. But, if you can pre-sell an additional 3000 units to three distributors for $3.00 each your unit cost may drop to $2.75, providing enough additional revenue to cover the freight to four locations (yours and the three distributors) and providing a lower unit cost to you.

But won't you find yourself in competition with these other three distributors when it comes time to sell your books?

This can be overcome by careful selection of distributors and prior agreement on promotional techniques. Many publishers are happy to acquire titles for promotion to their existing mailing list and to use as back-up offers to their current buyers. You can even benefit from any minor competition generated by this technique if you insert a return postcard (addressed to you, naturally) in each of your books entitling the buyer to a free catalog of your offerings. This gives you a limited access to other publisher's valuable mailing lists.

Finally, most reasonable publishers know that there is really nothing new under the sun. We all share the same basic pool of ideas and information. Publishing is merely the presentation and packaging of the information that is available to us all in one form or an other. Short of outright plagiarism we all borrow from our colleagues. Its a process called "learning." So why not formalize the process and help each other to gain mutual benefit? This is perhaps one of the aspects of publishing that confounds executives from other industries who are usually obsessed with secrecy and espionage. In practical fact, there is so much information to be disseminated to so many willing buyers that no reasonably creative publisher will ever saturate a market singlehandedly.

MAIL ORDER

One of the best and most cost effective sales techniques for the small publisher is *direct mail*. Because of the high value/cost ratio found in the book publishing industry self-published books lend themselves to this approach. It is commonly agreed that to be successful in direct mail marketing you must have a product that allows what retailers call a 67% mark-up. Because retailers determine mark-up percent on their retail price (not wholesale cost) this means they must sell a product for three times what it costs to achieve a 67% mark-up. Simply stated, the items that costs $10.00 must be sold for $30 via direct mail. This "triple your costs" rule is only an arbitrary minimum test for a pricing. In fact, you may choose to sell your book for much more if it contains valuable, wanted information.

value /cost ratio

Most books selling for $29.95 plus postage and handling (a very popular mail order book price) actually cost the publisher less than $5.00. In some cases, far less than $5.00. One problem with the direct mail book business is the flood of get-rich-quick schemers, selling worthless little pamphlets for exorbitant prices. Many people have been discouraged by this practice and resist ordering books by mail unless they are from well known publishers. This makes it doubly important for the new publisher to produce the highest quality products and represent himself in a serious non-sensational manner. Selling what cost you $5.00 (or even $3.50) for $29.95 is not excessive mark-up if your book is well written and packed with valuable information that will enhance people's lives. Most products we buy everyday carry a similar or greater mark-up. We are simply unaware of it because the increase between original product cost and retail price is shared by a number of wholesalers, jobbers and retailers. As a self publisher, you will be performing most of these functions.

Actually, you will not be pocketing your gross margin of $24.95 per sale ($29.95 less your cost of $5.00). Far from it, the cost of promotion will eat up a substantial portion of your gross margin and the typical shipping and handling charge of $3.00 is barely enough to cover those costs. Contrary to some beliefs, mail order is no get-rich-quick panacea. It requires the same diligence, attention to detail, and sound judgment that nurtures any enterprise. Given those elements, it can be very rewarding, especially since it can be started with a minimal investment.

direct mail
direct response
two step

There are three basic direct marketing approaches: direct mail, direct response advertising, and the two step method. Of the three, direct mail is by far the most expensive. It consists of renting the one-time use of a list of potential buyers from a competing publisher or the publisher of a magazine that targets an audience likely to be interested in your book. You then prepare a direct mail package consisting of: 1. a well written letter (usually 4 to 8 pages) that stresses the benefits the potential customer will receive from your book, 2. a brochure showing the book and highlighting it's features, 3. a reply card the customer can fill out to order, 4. a reply envelope, 5. a mailing envelope. Unless you are able to produce these packages in massive quantities (100,000 or more) your costs will look something like this:

Six page letter	$.18
Three panel two color brochure	.09
Reply envelope	.02

reply card	.0
List rental	.05
List management sort & stuff labor	.05
Second class postage	.18
TOTAL	$.58

cost of direct mail

This doesn't look like a bad investment to sell a $30.00 book. But, there's an important point most mail-order promoters fail to reveal. You can reasonably expect a response of 1% to 3% from your mailing. In fact, seasoned pros congratulate themselves on a well written job when they hit the 3% mark. Lets look at the impact of this startling revelation on a typical mailing of 1000 pieces:

Cost of Mailing 1000 pieces	588.00
3% response	30 sales
Gross income	988.50 (30 x $29.95 + $3.00 S&H)
Cost of books	150.00
Profit before taxes	217.50

Even though a major mailing requires a lot of effort, this is not a bad return on your money. But, look at what happens when response drops below the magic 3% mark.

Cost of Mailing 1000 pieces	588.00
2% response	20 sales
Gross income	659.00 (30 x 29.95 + 3.00 S&H)
Cost of books	100.00
Profit before taxes	-29.00

Why would anyone go to all that trouble to loose money, you could do it much faster in Atlantic City. The truth is, many mail order houses actually plan to loose money on their initial mailings because they want to build a valuable customer base of their own and believe they will more than recoup their losses on subsequent offerings to these same customers. In fact, may mail order authorities *back-up offers* say you should never run an ad or do a single mailing with only one product. To achieve true mail order success you must be able to offer your customer a second product when you deliver his first purchase. Think of your own experience, have you ever received a mail order purchase without also getting flyers or catalogs in the same package?

lift-notes In recent years many direct mail operators have used the **lift-note** or sealed envelope technique to raise response rates. This is simply a separate and smaller slip of colored paper, folded in half. The outside is printed with a message such as, "read my letter first" the inside of the folded slip contains a message about some further inducement, added bonus for ordering, or a limited time discount. The message is often hand written and sometimes sealed in a small envelope. Operators have reported that this technique adds mystery and interest to an offer and helps stress the value of bonus offers or special discounts. Frankly, it has been so over used that more sophisticated prospects will find it insulting. A strong, well composed sales letter that hammers away at the customer benefits your book will produce and ends with an added incentive (discount or unexpected bonus) will probably sell more books.

elements of asuccessful direct mail campaign Most mail order operators agree that the success of a mailing depends on these elements in descending order of importance:

1. *The Quality of the List.* Mediocre mailings to great list can be successful. But, great mailings to poor lists are doomed to failure. The test of a great list is in the answer to the following questions:

   A. Is this a list of buyers or a compiled list of names who have simply asked for information on a certain subject or product? You want lists of people who have actually bought books like yours through the mail.

   B. How old is the list? Lists age rapidly and retain little value after six months.

C. When did the names on the list make their last purchase? Names that have not made a purchase in 18 months should be culled from the list.

D. What was the size of the last purchase made? You should mail only to those names that have responded to an offer similar to yours. People who have purchased a $5.00 report are not good candidates for $99.00 directory offers.

E. Can I rent a small section of the list for a test mailing? List brokers who are unwilling to allow you to test 1500 to 2000 names are usually aware that their list is inappropriate to your needs or at least badly sorted and culled. Always test lists! Tests of less than 1500 are inconclusive and expensive. Ask that your test list be composed of the widest possible assortment of zip codes. This is a little more trouble for the broker but it will give you a more accurate test. Remember, you don't have to accept any existing list criteria. Computer maintained lists can be sorted for you by criteria you specify.
For instance, you may ask for;

    a. 1500 names

    b. no more than 5 names from any single zip code

    c. all people who have purchased books on gardening for $25 or more in the last 90 days.

2. *The Quality of the Letter.* Many books have been written on the subject of sales letters. One of the best is *Creating Direct Mail Letters* published by the Dartnell Corporation. This loose leaf volume contains a collection of outstanding direct mail letters prepared for some of America's largest and most prolific mailers along with commentary and tips from the top mail order pros. It

is available by mail order from; Dartnell, 117 West Micheltorena, Santa Barbara, CA 93101-9978. After an exhaustive study of the subject most professionals seem to agree on the following points:

A. Sales letters should look as much like personal letters as possible. Use the type face *Courier* or others that resemble typewriter type. Don't use a slick proportion-spaced type. Line spacing should be open and light. Don't try to pack the page. Use wide margins and paragraph indents.

B. Open your letter with large bold faced type that proclaims one or more of the major benefits of your book. This should precede the salutation.

C. Use a complimentary salutation appropriate to the people you are addressing, such as; "Dear Entrepreneur" or "Dear Sports Enthusiast" .

D. Continue to stress the benefits your book will provide in a bright, friendly, conversational tone. The text should read like a letter from an old friend who is excited to share a wonderful discovery with the reader. It should not sound like a high pressure sales letter.

E. Long letters work better than short letters. Allow yourself to repeat important benefits. State the same benefit in different terms. Never apologize for being redundant. Many good direct mail letters are 12 to 16 pages long.

F. Use hand written inserts underlining and arrows to emphasize important points. Print these in a second color (usually dark blue). This gives the page visual variety and stresses your sense of urgency. Even though the recipient knows they are reading a printed letter that was probably sent to thousands of others, the inclusion of these "personal touches" strengthens the perception of an important relationship between writer and reader.

G. Ask for the sale. Roughly 2/3 of the way through the letter you must make it clear what you want the reader to do. "Act now", "mail your order today." "Don't let another day pass without the benefits of this book." Use strong direct language to emphasize the action the reader must take to acquire the benefits you have described.

3. *The Appropriateness of the Offer* Every book (or product) has an **optimum rate of sale**. To achieve this optimum rate you must discover precisely the right promotional elements, all the factors we have been discussing; list, letter, envelope, timing, price. All these key elements must be precisely right for your book, not your last book but your current book. Few books share exactly the same sets of key elements. So how do you discover this Midas Touch in mail order? Through constant testing. Although there is no perfect formula, experienced mail order operators know the general range in which their tests should begin because they have specialized in one (or two) limited areas of interest. They know their customers, their book buying habits, their financial limits, the key phrases that push their customer's buy buttons.

Experienced mail order operators view every mailing as an opportunity to test one (and only one) key element of their offer. There a re few, if any non-test mailings. Even when these operators determine that a particular list is a winner and a large commitment has been made to mailing it, *split runs* will be used to test the other key elements such as price, letter, bonus offers, etc. They not only test for response but for profit margin.

Frequently a book will produce a significantly better profit if the price is reduced. By discovering the price at which the book sells best the publisher comes closer to the optimum rate of sale. The economy of scale he achieves allows the mail order publisher to cut printing costs and therefore improve margin in spite of the lower cost to the customer. This can, however, work in reverse. Specialized books that require a higher promotion-cost/sale ratio will frequently produce greater profit at a higher price and lower sales volume. Test your offer carefully to determine the correct price.

4. *The Timing of the Offer* Timing too plays a vital role in the perfect key element mix. Many books on mail order discuss the best and worst months to mail but these highly generalized conclusions can do more harm than good to the novice mail order publisher. Presumably July is a poor month. Everyone is on vacation and out of a buying mode. But, suppose your book concerns backyard construction projects, fly-casting techniques or preparing your garden for winter. July would be a great time to advertise. After the application of reasonable common sense, timing too must be subject to the same rigorous testing that you apply to other key elements. Effective direct response offers must be received early in any particular season, when people are just beginning to think about the activity your book covers. Although your fulfillment may be prompt, the general public perception of mail order is that receipt of your book will take between four and six weeks. Therefore, if you are selling a book on "How to Sharpen Skis" plan your ads and mailings in September, not December. Conversely, August would probably be too early to mail. The recipient would still be in a summer activity mode and unreceptive to your offer.

5. *The Effectiveness of the Envelope.* Again, we are sorry to report that there is no clear-cut formula for the design of a direct mail envelope, you must test to find the approach that works best for your offer. There are, however, two distinct schools of thought on the subject.

School one says; use a plain #10 envelope with nothing more than a person's name and return address, no company name.

Avoid address labels. Use hand-addressing or the new laser direct impression printing available at most mail houses. In this way the recipient will believe that the package is a personal letter and not junk mail. Some direct mail operators have gone as far as to use craft colored window envelopes like the ones used by the I.R.S. Their sales letter or coupon is printed on green safety (check) paper and folded so that the recipient's name and address appears in the window as it would on a tax refund check. Other mailers use monarch sized envelopes and hand addressing to make their package look like a greeting card or party invitation. These tricks undoubtedly buy the operators added seconds of attention and, if the initial lines of their sales offer are truly compelling, they might even result in added sales. However, we believe that they are just as likely to irritate the prospect and evoke an image of deceptiveness which will be difficult to overcome.

School two says; create a benefit oriented teaser envelope that the recipient can't resist opening. A typical example would be an envelope that had 48 point type saying: "LEARN HOW TO INCREASE YOUR I.Q. BY 20 POINTS IN ONE DAY," then 12 point type saying: "see page three of my enclosed letter." You might use as many of these teasers as the envelope will hold but be sure to deliver the resolution (answer) to the teaser in your sales letter. Some operators make the mistake of forcing the recipient buy their book to resolve the envelope teasers. This also aggravates the prospect and creates an air of distrust. It is better to give the prospect some small concession in return for their attention to your sales pitch. This will enhance the perception that you will give more than full value in fulfillment of the order.

Even with a well constructed package plus the added value of multiple future sales, direct mail promotion should probably be the second (or third) choice of the beginner. There is too much margin for error and direct mail promotion works best when you have established your own list of repeat customers. Mailing to a "house list" that you have cleaned and refined over a period of years can render a far higher response and profit.

THE AD ALTERNATIVE

Direct response advertising is a better choice for those who have a few dollars to spend and a couple months to wait. Magazines and tabloid newspapers are the best media for these offerings. Choose publications that carry several offers similar to yours. Don't be a pioneer, at least not at first. A magazine that carries a book publisher's ad for several months must be producing results for that publisher. Although many publishers insist that one and two page ads are necessary to sell books, small publishers have had success with ads as small as one quarter page. Ads that include a reply coupon almost always out pull non-coupon ads.

establish you own ad agency   Direct response ads should be run for three consecutive months to achieve maximum benefits. Many potential customers will not respond to an ad the first or even the second time they see it. Repeated exposure always enhances the response rate. You will also receive a more favorable rate from most publications for a three issue commitment. Establish a *house ad agency* and give it a name that is different from your regular publishing business. Create a simple letterhead for your new agency and request *rate cards* from all the magazines you are considering. When you place your ads use an *Insertion Order* (see appendix) and deduct a 15% agency commission. This savings can be substantial over a period of time and most publications will not question the deduction if you enclose a check with your order. Check the rate card to see if your publication offers a cash discount, this can provide added savings (usually 2%).

The cost and return you might expect from a typical direct response ad looks like this:

Cost of full page ad X 3 issues = $11400.00

Circulation (not readership) = 300,000

Cost per thousand = 12.70

average 3% response X 3 issues =   27000 sales

typical ad cost/response

$$X29.95$$

gross sales =   808,650.00

average 2.5% response X 3 issues = 22500 sales

$$X29.95$$

gross sales =   673,875.00

average 2% response X 3 issues =   18000 sales

$$X29.95$$

gross sales =   539,100.00

average 1.5% response X 3 issues = 13500 sales

$$X29.95$$

gross sales =   404,325.00

cost of books and fulfillment =   5.95

gross margin per sale =   24.00

net profit from ad run for

3 months at average 3% response = $636,600.00

net profit from ad run for

3 months at average 2.5% response =   528,600.00

net profit from ad run for

3 months at average 2% response =   420,600.00

net profit from ad run for

3 months at average 1.5% response =   312,600.00

Please beware! This is a highly idealized example of what might happen to an astute publisher who has done exhaustive testing to correctly identify his market and create a product precisely tailored to it's needs. This process takes years of study and preparation. None the less, results like these are quite possible.

DOING THE TWO STEP

By far the most flexible and cost effective direct marketing technique for the novice publisher is what has become known as the two step method. It involves placing small display and classified ads in periodicals that are appropriate to your book's market. The ads don't attempt to make the sale. It is very difficult to sell anything costing more than five dollars in a small ad. Before your prospect will invest $20 to $30 he will want more information than you can possibly provide in a small or classified ad. The ad can do little more than pique the prospect's interest.

A typical ad might read:
Make $100.00 per hour and up refinishing antiques at home.
Send #10 SASE for details; Parker, 210
Wildwood, Lincoln NB 60632

an ad to develop leads only
This is the ideal two-step ad. It attracts attention with it's exciting lead statement. It qualifies the prospect by telling what the program is all about. It tells the prospect exactly what he must do to acquire these benefits and it does it in 20 words (most publications don't charge for ZIP Codes). Now all that is left to do is insert your sales package (same as discussed in direct mail section) in the respondent's self-addressed stamped envelope, drop it in the mail and wait for the order.

use voice mail to capture leads
Many publishers have used the new voice-mail response systems with some degree of success. Instead of sending a self addressed envelope for the sales package, the prospect calls an 800 number to hear your sales message. At the end of your message you can give the caller two options. Ask them for an order with their credit card or ask for their name and address so you can send written information and an order form.

The advantages of the voice-mail system are:

1. It's easier for your prospect to respond. No hunting for an envelope and stamp, just pick up the phone. There isn't even a charge for the call.

2. You'll save a little money on each ad because you won't need a long reply address. Most publications treat a phone number as one word.

3. The rapid response will improve your cash flow.

4. You'll experience a small savings in the cost of your mailing materials when people give you their orders on-line.

The disadvantages of the voice-mail system are:

1. It's easier for your prospect to respond. No hunting for an envelope and stamp, just pick up the phone. There isn't even a charge for the call. Unfortunately, this encourages the merely curious who send for everything that's free. Having to send a stamp and envelope helps to qualify your prospect to some degree. You'll get more inquiries with voice-mail, but not necessarily more orders.

2. Voice mail isn't all that cheep. You'll incur an average cost of three dollars per inquiry for just the voice mail service and your monthly 800 charges.

3. Most people are concerned about credit card fraud and won't give the necessary information to a voice mail system. Some voice -mail operators allow the caller the option of choosing a live operator to take their order. This seems to get a higher rate of response, but naturally there is an added cost to you for this service.

Some direct response promoters even claim that they have had success using simple answering machines on their home phone lines. It is highly questionable that many callers would leave their credit card information on a stranger's answering machine. But, this could be a low cost way to generate leads for mailing direct response packages. Whether you use voice-mail or an answering machine, your outgoing message should be as carefully composed and produced as a mailing piece. It must do more than simply lead into the prospect's response, it should be used as a benefit rich sales opportunity itself.

Notice how this typical script reinforces the prospect for calling and offerers additional benefits of ordering:

voice mail script   Thank you for calling DataMarket Incorporated, publishers of the amazing *Work At Home Business Directory*. Do you want to make $200.00 per week, $500.00 per week, even $2000.00 per week, right in the comfort of your own home? You can with the amazing *Work-At-Home Business Directory*. In it, you will find over 10,000 listings of companies that offer special opportunities for independent contractors who work at home in their spare time, making crafts, writing reports, compiling information and mailing letters. Some of these opportunities require easy-to-master skills. Other are so basic that anyone can take advantage of them, even the physically handicapped. With 10,000 opportunities from which to choose you will certainly find one that ideally suits your skills and interests.

Think about the freedom of earning a full-time income, right from your home. In most cases you can set your own hours, work as much or as little as you like. You'll have more time to spend with your family and friends, and your earnings will make the good-times more enjoyable.

Don't hesitate another day. Leave your credit card order at the end of this message and we'll include two important free bonuses:

First, well give your our iron-clad, money back guarantee. You must be totally satisfied with the *Work-At-Home Business Directory* or return it for a full refund any time, up to an entire year. Second, we'll send you a copy of our latest report, *How to Start and Succeed in Your*

Home Business. This report covers every aspect of developing a highly profitable home business. Special features include:

• How to purchase the most effective computer system for your needs. Spend a few hundred dollars on computers and get the benefits of an entire staff of employees.

• How to deal with taxes the fast and simple way. Don't become a slave to the government. Make your home-based business the most powerful tax advantage ever conceived. You'll save thousands.

• How to structure your day for maximum productivity, leaving you more hours to spend with family and friends.

This report alone would be worth the modest price of our directory, but its actually free when you order the *Work-At-Home Business Directory* for the low price of $29.95 including shipping and handling, and the report is your's to keep, even if you return the directory. Get ready now to leave your name, street address, credit card number and expiration date at the tone. We look forward to sending you this valuable tool that will put you on the road to financial freedom, at home. If you would like more information before ordering, send a self addressed stamped envelope to Home Business Directory, P.O. Box 2310, Farmingdale, New Jersey 07737. That address again is Home Business Directory, P.O. Box 2310, Farmingdale, New Jersey 07737.

Now, here's the tone.

MAKING IT REAL

There are several simple steps that lend credibility to your book and prepare it for the widest possible distribution. Most of these should be started before the completion of your manuscript. Even if you expect your primary channel of distribution is to be mail order, you should prepare your book for retail distribution by applying for a ISBN or International Standard Book Number. This number appears on the title page and back cover of virtually every book distributed in retail book stores. It is used by large book distributors as a means of identifying each edition of each titles and it is used by most large book store chains as the basis of their bar code stock control system. A new ISBN is issued each time a work is reissued or has it's binding changed. To obtain a ISBN you must write to R.R. Bowker (resource section) and ask for an application. The cost is $100 ($150 for rush service). You will be assigned a block of numbers you may apply to subsequent editions or titles.

While you're communicating with Bowker you might also apply for a SAN or Standard Address Number. This identifies most every publisher, wholesaler, bookstore, and library in the book industry. It has substantially aided the automation of book distributing. R.R. Bowker also publishes the massive *BOOKS IN PRINT*. This is considered the definitive "book finder" by most librarians and retailers. The major volume is published every November and it has spawned several lesser sub-directories. To register your creation in *BOOKS IN*

PRINT, ask the ABI (Advanced Book Information) Department at Bowker for their ABI Guide Book and several ABI forms. These forms should be filed about six months prior to publication. Once listed you can expect to receive an updated computer print-out six times a year. You must return this document with any changes in the status of your books. Failure to return it may jeopardize your listing.

Unlike the ISBN number, the LC or Library of Congress number identifies a particular work, not necessarily a specific edition or binding of that work. The function of the *Cataloging in Publication Office of the Library of Congress* is to lend order to a rather disorganized industry. It determines the correct catalog position of thousands of books from hundreds of publishers annually, prints catalog cards for subscriber libraries (practically every important one in the country) and disseminates information to libraries on new publications. Obtaining an LC number is essential if you want to sell your book to libraries. About 20,000 institutions around the world subscribe to the Library of Congress catalog card service. Some purchase every book cataloged. The LC number allows local librarians to order cards without a search fee. Numbers must be assigned prior to publication and the Library will grant numbers only to books they expect to include in their collection, or for which they anticipate substantial demand. This excludes many forms of light fiction, correspondence school lessons, teachers manuals, booklets of less than 50 pages, most sermons and publications from vanity presses.

Library of Congress numbering

There is no fee for the Library of Congress catalog number. New publishers must simply write to the Cataloging in Publication Office, Library of Congress, Washington, DC 20540 and ask for "Procedures for Securing Preassigned Library of Congress Catalog Card Numbers" and the appropriate "Request for Preassignment of LCC Number" application form 607-7. When you receive your LC number have it printed on the copyright page of your book and send a complimentary copy to the Library of Congress. They will provide a prepaid mailer. The book should arrive prior to your official publication date so that final cataloging can take place and the subscriber cards can be printed in time for your release. As an added benefit for your trouble your book will probably be included in *The National Union Catalog.* This is issued several times a year to most public and private libraries.

A second service of the Library of Congress is the provision of the *Cataloging in Publication* number block. These secondary numbers are also printed on the copyright page and help librarians shelve your volume correctly. Because of recent funding cuts, this service has been rather slow and unreliable so the private library supplier Quality Books has been filling the void. For $30 they will send you a data block which you may include on your copyright page. Contact Quality Books, 918 Sherwood Drive, Lake Bluff, IL 60044-220 4 or call them at (708) 295-2010, FAX (708)295-1556.

International Standard Serial Numbers   Yet another function of the Library of Congress is the issuing of *International Standard Serial Numbers* or ISSN. These should not be confused with ISBN numbers issued by R.R. Bowker. ISSN numbers are usually assigned to periodicals, (i.e. magazines, newspapers, newsletters, annuals or anything published in an infinite series). However, if you expect to update and reissue your book every three years or less, you should also apply for a ISSN. Request form 67-60 from the Library of Congress, National Serials Data Program, Washington, D.C. 20540.

If it seems as though all this registration and cataloging is a bit cumbersome for the self-publisher who simply wants to do a little mail order business, the pay-off will be increased credibility. Even if you never sold a single volume to a library, you will be taken more seriously by distributors and retail customers if you make an effort to acquire the trappings of a serious publisher. Avoid using the same name in the publisher's and author's slot on your book and on applications. Although your self-publishing enterprise will be perfectly legitimate, many people in the industry still confuse self-publishing with the old practice of *vanity presses.* These companies still exist to print (and presumably distribute) books for authors who pay for the service (because they can't get a real publisher interested in their project). Vanity presses are considered the vultures of the publishing industry. Their products are shunned by reviewers, distributors and libraries. You should avoid this stigma like the plague.

avoiding the "vanity" stegma

By all means, don't forget the most important registration of all, copyright. All books that are printed and all copies of your manuscript should have a copyright notice on the title page. A copyright notice consists of

copyright

© 1993 Pacific Learning Council, all rights reserved

The name appearing on the copyright notice may be that of the author, the publisher, or any individual or organization that owns the right to reproduce the book. For a more detailed discussion of this legal issue you should request Circular R1 *Copyright Basics* from the Register of Copyright, Library of Congress, Washington, DC 20559. At the same time request Form TX to register your book. Return the completed form along with two copies of your book and a $20 registration fee. This should be done no later than 90 days from the first printing of the book.

SUMMERY

The technology of desktop publishing continues to expand our horizons by allowing individuals to communicate on a level of sophistication once achieved by only large corporations and government. We hope we have offered some useful suggestion on how this technology can be employed. More important, we hope we have provoked some original thinking on your part. Nothing would delight us more than a letter from you that told how you had improved our idea or how you were inspired to develop an entirely new application for desktop publishing.

As we exploit this technology it is important for each of us to understand the awesome power our culture has vested in the printed word and apply this power prudently, constructively and with an appreciation for the value of an idea. Publishing, like practically every other industry, consumes both the physical resources of our planet and the attention of it's inhabitants. The ideas we disseminate should be worthy of both. For the publisher who has doubts about the value of his manuscript, restraint is the greatest virtue.

STANDARDS & PROCEEDURES

Developing a comprehensive standards and proceedures manual is one of the most effective ways to define responsibilities, outline acceptable performance and avoid conflict in a partnership or firm. It serves to remind partners and their employees alike; what is expected of them and how to handle the day to day operations of the company. these manuals are most effective when they deal simply and directly with real situations that occur repetitively in the course of business.

The following is offered as a possible basis for such a manual. Naturally it must be tailored to the needs of each user, but this one has served us well and is an integeral part of our partnership agreement.

OBJECTIVE

Company Name is organized as a partnership for the purpose of generating profit through the sale of printing and print-related services. It uses the knowledge and resources of the principals to acquire printing and services at the lowest possible price, then resell them to businesses and organizations.

It is our objective to give our customers fair value for the services they purchase, while making it easy for the average business person to access state-of-the-art printing technology. We distinguish our services from conventional "desk-top-publishers" by providing design and marketing in-put, suggesting more effective marketing techniques, and helping our clients produce unique marketing vehicles. By providing these value-added services we will capture clients who's requirements are too sophisticated for franchised print-shops yet not complex enough to warrant the attention of a full service advertising agency.

We are happy to print completed mechanicals delivered to us in any conventional form. We recognize that our highest profits per hour will be achieved when alterations to the client's existing material is minimized. However, we offer clients the ability to alter their materials as needed or generate entirely new designs. Offers to alter a client's materials are effective marketing tools in two instances:

1. When it is apparent that the client will be disappointed by printing of the existing mechanicals.

2. When it is apparent that a client is "shopping for price" we are in a position to offer value-added service beyond the ability of the franchised or store-front printer, thus securing the job without excessive price concessions.

Company Name offers the following services:

1. Analysis of a client's printing needs. By carefully reviewing a client's plans we determine if previous printings were cost effective and we show the client alternatives that will produce better results at the same or lower cost.

2. Acquisition of photographic services. By using local photographers, production studios and various forms of stock photography we provide the best cost/value ratio in the photo-buying process. Furthermore, because we are managing the entire project we will assure that all photography will be appropriate (both aesthetically and mechanically) to the end product.

3. Photo manipulation. Through the use of digital processes we are able to enhance and manipulate a client's photography. Although this service is not a high-margin profit center in itself, it can provide important leverage in acquiring jobs that might otherwise go to conventional print-shops or photographer-broker organizations.

4. Illustration. The generation of simple charts, graphs, cartoons, line illustrations will be done in-house and billed at the prevailing rate. Although this service is not a high-margin profit center in itself, it can provide important leverage in acquiring jobs that might otherwise go to conventional print-shops or photographer-broker organizations. More complex or stylized illustration will be subcontracted and the cost, plus a predetermined mark-up passed on to the client.

5. Design. Although the majority of projects we accept are fairly straightforward, some will require a degree of stylization. Although this service is not a high-margin profit center in itself, it can provide important leverage in acquiring jobs that might otherwise go to conventional print-shops or photographer-broker organizations.

6. *Mechanical preparation.* The assembly of text, forms, charts, photography and illustration in the most attractive and cost-effective printing format is central to our ability to acquire business.

7. *Printing Management.* Using our extensive resources we will select the printer who's equipment and schedule best fit each project. In most cases, we will acquire competitive bids, place printing orders, monitor bluelines and making press checks as necessary. We will arrange for the product to be delivered to the client.

Additionally, we may, from time to time, offer concept and copy development in an effort to acquire a particularly attractive job that carries a high profit potential. The client, however, must accept the ultimate responsibility for all copy and proofing, per our contract.

OPERATIONAL PROCEDURES

To lend order to the operation of our business and assure maximum profitability it is agreed that we will establish specific standards for operation. These are designed to protect the client's interest as well as our own.

1. *Review of new projects.* All new projects must be reviewed by one of the partners who will assess it's suitability for the firm. Projects determined to be too small, too complex or too large for us to handle profitably will be declined. No representations or assurances made to clients or potential clients are binding on the firm until the specific project has been reviewed *by both partners* and a written proposal has been issued. Special care will be given to projects with unusually short deadlines. These are the projects most likely to incur rush charges, generate mistakes and cause loss of profit.

1A. All new projects accepted will be assigned a consecutive job number. This number with a brief detail of the job, the due date, the client and the status will be published on a *Job List*. Jobs remain on the Job List until they are invoiced or otherwise terminated. The Job List is updated weekly. All purchase orders, transmittals and invoices pertaining to the job must reference the job number. In this way, it is possible for everyone in the office to quickly and accurately identify a project, answer client's questions and assign costs. Job numbers also avoid confusion between jobs that may naturally bare similar or identical titles.

2. *Proposals.* Upon acceptance of a project one or more partners will supervise the preparation of a proposal to the client. Each proposal will clearly delineate the services to be performed and the quantity and quality of printing to be produced. The purpose of the proposal is to convey to the client precisely what we will do and what it will cost. There should be no ambiguity in a proposal. Any deviation from normal procedure should be clearly stated. For instance, it is standard procedure to obtain drum scans from a service bureau for all reproduction of color photos. If we determine that it is more important to reduce the mechanical costs of a job by using in-house flat-bed scans the client should be so advised. Similarly, the use of below-normal grade paper, the use of a clients substandard photos or any other factor that could result in client dissatisfaction must be clearly stated in the proposal.

2A. A secondary purpose of a proposal is to aid in finalizing the sale. Inclusion of specific client requests and mention of additional features in the *job description* section helps the client understand that they are receiving a custom product, tailored to their specific needs by professionals.

2B. The standard designer and printer terms included in the appendix of this document will become a part of every proposal and clients will be encouraged to read and understand them.

2C. All clients will be required to make a deposit to begin their initial project. The customary deposit is one third the total amount of the proposed total. Exceptions may be made upon mutual agreement of the partners. The primary reason for making an exception to the "one third rule" is a client's particularly good (or poor) credit history.

2D. All propoals must be approved by both partners and signed by one. Upon signing the proposal, the responsible partner will ensure that a copy is placed in the *Active Proposal Book* so that anyone in the office can refer to the document and answer questions regarding it. The client is given two copies of the proposal, one for them to sign and return to us and one for their file.

2E. Prior to the issuance of a proposal the partners will decide who will act as *project manager* for the job. The project manager is responsible for keeping the job on time and on budget. They are also responsible for informing the other partner when their assistance will be required on the job and how they are expected to perform.

2Ea. The project manager will assess the extent of the job and determine if it is necessary to issue a time and action calendar in conjunction with the proposal. It is generally considered advisable to make such a calendar an integral part of complex project proposals

2F. No project will be undertaken until the client signs and returns a copy of the proposal with the appropriate deposit.

3. *Purchase Orders.* All orders that result in the commitment of funds or credit in excess of $150. must be made in the form of a numbered purchase order. Purchase orders will be reviewed by both partners. The purpose of this review is:

   A. to attempt to devise more cost-effective techniques to accomplish the same ends.

   B. to check for potential errors that may add additional cost to the job.
A copy of the standard purchase order is found in the appendix.

3A. Whenever it is necessary to send transportable media (such as Syquest Disks) out of the office, a notation should be made in the *enclosures* section of the purchase order or transmittal. An additional copy of the document should be placed in a special *Media In/Out File* to be maintained by each project manager. When media is returned the copy is simply discarded. Contractors or clients who fail to return media will be billed at our cost plus 30%.

3B. The *insertion order* is a variation on the purchase order. It is used when placing an ad with print media and it accommodates the usual discounts given to agencies. The same rule of review applies to insertion orders.

4. *Job Folders.* Every job, (including all but the simplest proposals) requires a job folder. A copy of every document relating to a job will be placed in the job folder regardless of whether it was generated by this firm or received by this firm. Examples of documents to be filed in the job folder include;

    all versions of a proposal

    all transmittals

    all notations of conversations with clients

    all proofs submitted to clients

    all requests for quotation

    all quotations

    all original photographs or illustrations

The purpose of the job folder is to enable any individual to understand, and if necessary, continue a job that has been previously managed by another person, thus providing clients with accurate and seamless service.

4A. Job folders will be located in a designated place on the project manager's desk while the job remains active. After invoicing the folder will be filed in the company archives under the client's name.

4B. Frequently large projects will become too bulky for simple folders. In this case we will use expanding or accordion file folders with compartments that can be labeled by category of document or contents.

4C. Items such as composite film and mechanicals will be placed in clearly marked portfolios or film boxes and stored in the standing flat-file. Labels should indicate the project's name, completion date and job number.

5. *Proofing. Accuracy* is a vital element of customer service. Nothing is more likely to alienate a client than common errors in copy, spelling punctuation, grammar or typographic alignment. Unfortunately, these errors are easy to make and often hard to detect. What's more, clients usually take the position that errors are the responsibility of the designer. Even if the client provided the final draft of their copy on disk, they expect the designer to proof for other than technical errors. For these reasons we will take the following steps to ensure client satisfaction.

5A. No rough or proof will be presented before both a spell check and a grammar check program is run on the work.

5B. At least one partner and one other person must review all roughs and proofs prior to client presentation.

5C. Whenever possible, roughs and proofs should be allowed to "sit" overnight for a fresh review the following day.

5D. Although it is no substitute for meticulous proofing, the client must sign a release form prior to the generation of any film. This release simply states that they have been shown laser-copy roughs of their project and that, as far as they can tell, it is satisfactory. Copy changes or ACs made after the client signs the release will be billed to the client at prevailing rates. However, we will bare part of the cost of film regeneration (in the interest of client satisfaction) if we make mistakes that both we and the client fail to discover before the generation of film.

5E. Clients will be required to sign a second release prior to printing. This release indicates that they have been shown color proofs or bluelines and that all copy and color renditions are acceptable. Should the client be unavailable to sign this release, they may sign a waver form indicating that they accept the judgement of this firm concerning these matters. Both releases and the waver form are found in the appendix.

5F. No project will be delivered to a client without copies being sent to this office. Ideally, projects should be delivered here prior to the delivery to clients. This is not always possible, however, we must never be placed in the position of fielding client comments or complaints without having copies of the product to which we can refer.

6. *Assignment of partner responsibility.* To avoid duplication of effort and maximize the talent and abilities of the partners, certain billable and non-billable duties are pre-assigned to the partners as follows:

6A. Accounting and tax preparation including management of accounts payable and receivable is the responsibility of *Partner A*. He will make every reasonable effort to communicate his decisions with *Partner B* and ask for input on policy matters.

6B. Client contact and sales is the primary responsibility of *Partner B*. This includes the development of promotional programs, drafting letters to prospective clients and meeting with prospects.

6C. Decisions concerning the purchase and implementation of new hardware and software are made by *Partner A*.

6D. Primary design and copy decisions are made by *Partner B*.

6E. Primary decisions concerning the preparation of documents for printing are made by *Partner B*.

6F. Work required to maintain or improve the physical condition of the office will be the responsibility of both partners.

6F. Both partners will be jointly responsible for the following duties to be performed as the need arises:
  a. generation of proposals
  b. development of requests for quotation
  c. maintenance of resource files.

It is agreed that the partners will remain flexible in the execution of all duties and never allow these designations to interfere with effective customer service.

7. *Ownership of accounts.* It is acknowledged that only accounts acquired through mutually agreed and funded promotions will be owned by the partnership. Regardless of the scope of these accounts, business generated from personal or institutional contacts gained through joint promotion will be considered the property of the partnership.

7A. Subject to the agreement of both partners, we may elect to bring a particular project or account into the partnership in order to provide more effective client service, financial support, technical or design expertise. The partnership will have no claim on the account or future business with the client as long as this project or account was not related to a partnership promotion.

7B. Neither partner shares any responsibility for projects, clients, businesses, investments, invoices, contracts or commitments made by the other partner, except for those relating directly to partnership-owned project.

8. The resources and contractors used by the partnership constitute a valuable asset which is regularly resold to our clients for profit. No resource is divulged to a client and no direct client resource is ever encouraged.

8A. Only resources (i.e. printers, binderies, prepress service bureaus, fabricaters, etc.) that agree to protect the ownership of our accounts will be utilized. Resources who ship directly to our clients will be provided with labels and packing slips with *Our Company Name* imprinted on them.

DESKTOP PUBLISHING RESOURCES

The following resources are presented as representative of those available to the desktop publishing industry. It is not intended to be a comprehensive list of any category, nor does inclusion imply any endorsement of the resource.

ASSOCIATIONS

American Society for Information Science 1424 16th Street N.W., Suite 404, Washington, DC 20001, phone (202) 462-10000.

Association for Computing Machinery 11 West 42nd Street, New York, NY 10036, phone (212) 869-7440.

Copyright Clearance Center, Inc. 27 Congress Street, Salem, MA 01970, phone (617) 744-3350.

Independent Computer Consultants Association P.O. Box 27412, St. Louis, MO 63141, phone (314) 997-4633.

Information Industry Association 555 New Jersey Avenue N.W., Suite 800, Washington, DC 20001, phone (202) 639-8262.

National Association of Desktop Publishers (NADTP) c/o Venture Communications, 60 Madison Avenue, New York, NY 10160.

BOOK DUMPS

ABEL Express, 230 East Main Street, Carnegie, PA 15106, phone (412) 279-0672.

Alpak Manufacturing, 185 Route 17, Mahwah, NJ 07430, phone (201) 529-4444.

City Diecutting, Inc, 17 Cotters Lane, East Brunswick, NJ 08816, phone (908) 390-9599, fax (908) 390-8654.

BOOK DESIGN

Comp-Type Inc, 155 Cypress Street, Fort Bragg, CA 95437, phone (707) 964-9520, fax (707) 964-7531.

Design Etc., 7738 Post Road, Winston, GA 30187, phone (404) 942-5797, fax (404) 920-0729.

Desktop Studio, 290 Larkspur Plaza Drive, Larkspur, CA 94939, phone (415) 924-8036.

Didona Design Associates, phone (800) 786-3010.

Dunn+Associates Advertising Design, phone (715) 634-4857.

Graffolio, 1528 Mississippi Street, La Crosse, WI 54601, phone (608) 784-8064.

Robert Howard, 631 Mansfield Drive, Fort Collins, CO 80525 phone (303) 225-0083.

Lightbourne Images, phone (800) 697-9833.

Pacific Design Group, 251 Post Street, San Francisco, CA 94108, phone (415) 391-4135, fax (415) 788-5738.

Carolyn Porter, 7944 Capistrano Avenue, West Hills, CA 91304-4603, phone/fax (818) 340-6620.

Cristina C. Santos, 11755 Slauson Avenue, Suite B, Santa Fe Springs, CA 90670, phone/fax (310) 695-1555.

BOOK PRINTERS

Adams Press, 25 East Washington Street, Chicago, IL 60602, phone (312) 676-3426.

American Offset Printing, 3600 South Hill Street, Los Angeles, CA 90007, phone (213) 231-4133.

Andrews Printing Co., Inc., 2141 Bixby Road Lakewood, CA 90712, (310) 426-7123, (800) 266-7123.

Arrow Graphics, Inc., P.O. Box 291, Cambridge, MA 02238, phone (617) 926-8585, fax (617) 926-0982.

George Banta Co., Curtis Reed Plaza, Menasha, WI 54942, phone (414) 722-7771, (800) 722-3324.

Bawden Printing, Inc., 400 South 14th Avenue, Eldridge, LA 52748, fax (319-285-4828, *Has local representatives in many areas.*

BookCrafters, 613 Industrial Drive, Chelsea, MI 48118, phone (313) 475-9145, fax (313) 475-7337.

BookMasters, 638 Jefferson Street, Ashland, OH 44805 (800) 537-6727, (419) 281-1731, *Will typeset, print, store, take orders via 800#, pack and ship your books.*

Book Mart Press, 2001 Forty Second Street, North Bergen, NJ, (201) 864-1887.

Book Press, Putney Road, Brattleboro, VT 05201, phone (802) 257-7701 (800) 732-7310.

Braun-Brumfield, P.O. Box 1203, Ann Arbor, MI 48106, phone (313) 662-3291.

Century Graphics, 1013 McDermott Road, Metaire, LA 70001, fax (510) 834-3086.

Crane Duplicating Services, Inc., 1611 Main Street, West Barnstable, MA 02668, fax (518) 362-5445.

Cushing-Malloy, P.O. Box 8632, Ann Arbor, MI 48107, phone (313) 663-8554.

Delta Electronic Publishing, 28210 N.Avenue Stanford, Velencia, CA 91355-1111, fax (805) 257-3867.

R.R. Donnelley & Sons, 2223 Martin Luther King Drive, Chicago, IL 60616, phone (800) 428-0832, (312) 993-7555, *Huge book and magazine printer, good for long runs, many plants all over country.*

Flambeau Litho Corporation, Highway 8 East, Tony, WI 54563, phone (800) 255-9929, (715) 322-5268.

Gilliland Printing, Inc., 215 Summit, Arkansas City, KS 67005, phone (800) 332-8200, fax (316) 442-8504.

Graphic Illusions, 17 Shad Hole Road, Dennisport, MA 02639-0020, phone (508) 760-1321, fax (508) 760-2506.

Griffin Printing, 544 West Colorado Street, Glendale, CA 91204-1102, phone (800) 826-4849 in California (800) 423-5789.

Graham Printing, 17475 Gale Avenue, Rowland Heights, CA 91748-1515, phone (818) 964-7354.

GRT Book Printing, 3960 East 14th Street, Oakland, CA 94601, phone (510) 534-5032, fax (510) 534-1873. *Specializing in short run, black and white books and manuals.*

Harlo Press, 50 Victor Avenue, Detroit, MI 48203, phone (313) 883-3600.

Hearth Publishing, 16731 East Illiff, Aurora, CO 80013, fax (303) 751-5455.

Jostens Printing & Publishing, P.O. Box 991, Visalia, CA 93279, phone (209) 651-3300.

Kimberly Press, 5390 P Overoass Road, Santa Barbara, CA 93111-2008, phone (805) 964-6469.

KNI, Incorporated, 1261 South State College Parkway, Anaheim, CA 92806, fax (714) 635-1744.

W.A. Krueger Co., 2115 East Kansas City Road, Olathe, KS 66061, phone (913) 764-5600.

Marrakech Express, 500 Anclote Road, Tarpon Springs, Fl 34689-6701, fax (813) 937-4758.

MBP Lithographics, 135 North Maion Street, Hillsboro, KS 67063, fax (316) 947-3392.

McNaughton & Gunn, Inc., P.O. Box 10, Saline, MI 48176, fax (800) 677-2665.

Media Publications, 3050 Coronado Drive, Santa Clara, CA 95054, fax (408) 492-0475.

Morgan Printing & Publishing, 900 Old Koenig Lane, Austin, TX 78756, phone (512) 459-5194.

Odyssey Press Inc., 133 Crosby Road, Dover, NH 03820-4376, phone (603) 749-4433, fax (603) 749-1425.

Omnipress, P.O. Box 7125, Madison, WI 53791, (800) 828-0305, (608) 257-7275.

Patson's Press, 508 Tasman Drive, Sunnyvale, CA 94089, fax (408) 747-0512.

Patterson Printing, 1550 Territorial Road, Benton Harbor, MI 49022, phone (800) 848-8826, (616) 925-2177, fax (616) 925-6057.

Printright- Hong Kong, fax (805) 943-7241, *Broker for Hong Kong printers, appropriate for larger runs or color work.*

Publishers Press, 1900 West 2300 South, Salt Lake City, UT 84119, phone (801) 972-6600.

Publishing & Printing, 3102 Scaad Road, Knoxville, TN 37921, (615) 947-3575, *low price for cold web printed books.*

Rose Printing, P.O. Box 5078, Tallahassee, FL 32314, phone (800) 227-3725, (904) 576-4151.

Separacolor International, phone (800) 779-1158, (310) 608-0011 fax (310) 608-5862 *Specializes in color separations and color printing in Singapore.*

Spilman Printing, 1801 Ninth Street, Sacramento, CA 95814, phone (916) 448-3511, (800) 448-3511.

Thomason-Shore, Inc., 7300 P West Joy Road, Dexter, MI 48130-0305, phone (313) 426-3939.

Triangle Printing, P.O. Box 100854, Nashville, TN 37224, fax (800) 845-4767.

Vaughan Printing, 411 Cowan Street, Nashville, TN 37207, phone (615) 256-2244.

Viking Press, 7000 Washington Avenue South, Eden Prairie, MN 55344, phone (800) 328-7327, (612) 941-8780.

Walsworth Publishing Co., 306 North Kansas Avenue, Marceline, MO 64658, phone (816) 376-3543.

Whitehall Company, 1200 South Willis Avenue, Wheeling, IL 60090, phone (312) 541-9290, fax (312) 541-5890.

CD ROM PHOTOS
Creative Data, Inc., phone (800) 237-6654, *great selection of stock photos on disk for as little as $99.95 includes repro-rights.*

PhotoDisc Inc., 2013 Fourth Street, Seattle, WA 98121, phone (206) 441-9355, fax (206) 441-9379, *great collections of stock photos on CD, sold with repro rights, very reasonable.*

CLIP ART
3G Graphics Inc., 114 Second Avenue, Edmonds, WA 98020, phone (800) 456-0234.

Arro International, P.O. Box 167, Montclair, NJ 07042, phone (800) 243-1515, (201) 746-9620, fax(201) 509-0728.

AdArt, phone 41 Mansfield Avenue, Essex Junction, VT 05452, phone (800) 255-0562, fax (802)878-1768.
Artbeats, phone (800) 444-9392, (503) 863-4428, *great full color background patterns and textures on disk.*

Art Parts, P.O. Box 2926, Orange, CA 92669-0926, phone (714) 633-9617.

Bruce Jones Design Inc., 31 St. James Avenue, Boston, MA 02116, phone (617) 350-6160, fax (617) 350-8764, *maps, ready to use or easy to customize.*

Cartesia Software, 5 South Main Street, Lambertville, NJ 08530, phone (609) 397-1611, fax (609) 397-5724, *maps on disk.*

Clipables, phone (800) 288-7585.

Dream Maker Software, 925 West Kenyon Avenue, #16 Englewood, CO 80110, phone (303)762-1001, fax (303) 762-0762.

Discount Clip Art, phone(800) 455-4278

Federal Clip Art, 7011 Evergreen Court, Annandale, VA 22003, phone (800) 258-5280, (703) 642-1177, fax (703) 642-9088, *government seals and military clip art.*

MediClip, phone (310) 315-3470, *medical illustrations on disk.*

Metro ImageBase, Inc., 18623 Ventura Blvd., Suite 210, Tarzana, CA 91356, phone (800) 525-1552, *collections of EPS images on CD.*

PolyType, 12003 Santa Monica Blvd., Los Angles, CA 90025, phone (800) 998-9934, (310) 444-9934, fax (310) 444-7897, *symbols and clip art as readily accessible fonts .*

ProArt, phone (800) 447-1950, *collections of EPS images on disk.*

TechPool Studios, 1463 Warrensville Center Road, Cleveland OH 44121, phone (800) 777-8930. *medical illustrations on disk.*

Dover Publications, Inc., 31 East 2nd Street, Mineola, NY 11501, *great collection of paperback books of scanable line art.*

Dynamic Graphics, Inc., 6000 North Forest Park Drive, Peoria, IL 61656-1901, phone (800) 255-8800, *great quality, comprehensive subscription program, both reflective and data on disk versions.*

Totem Graphics, Inc., 6200-F Capitol Blvd., Tumwater, WA 98501-5288, phone (206) 352-1851, fax (206) 352-2554. *collections of EPS images on disk.*

COMMISSIONED BOOK REPRESENTATIVES
The Publishers Book Exhibit, 86 Milwood Road, Milwood, NY 10546, phone (914) 762-2422 .

The Conference Book Service, Inc. 80 South Early Street, Alexandra, VA 22304, phone (703) 823-6968.

Quality Books, 918 Sherwood Drive, Lake Bluff, IL 60044-2204, phone (312) 295-2010. *Specializes in sales to libraries.*

COMPUTER HARDWARE & SOFTWARE DISCOUNTERS
APS Technologies, 6131 Deramus, Kansas City, MO 64120, phone (800) 235-3707, *systems and peripherals.*

Bottom Line, 1219 West 6th Street, Austin, TX 78703, phone (800) 235-9748, (512) 472-4956, *systems and peripherals.*

Club Mac, 7 Hammond, Irvine, CA 92718, phone (800) 258-2622, *peripherals.*

Data Comm Warehouse, P.O. Box 301, 1720 Oak Street, Lakewood, NJ 08701-9885, phone (800) 328-2261.

DrMac, 11050 Randall Street, Sun Valley, CA 91352, phone (800) 825-6227.

DTP Desktop Publishing Direct, 5198 West 76th Street, Edina, MN 55439, phone (800) 395-7778.

Hardware That Fits, 610 South Frazier, Conroe, TX 77301, phone (800) 364-3487.

INMAC, 2300 Valley View Lane, Irving, TX 75062-5058, phone (800) 547-5444.

Tiger Software, 800 Douglas Entrance, Executive Tower, 7th floor, Coral Gables, FL 33134, phone (800) 666-2562.

MacConnection, 14 Mill Street, Marlow, NH 03456, phone (800) 800-2222.

MacMall, phone (800) 222-2808, *systems and peripherals.*

Mac News, 1555 Sherman Avenue, Suite 361, Evenston, IL 60201, phone (800) 723-7755, *peripherals.*

Mac's Place, 100 Financial Drive, Kalispell, MT 59901, phone (800) 895-0009.

MacProducts USA, 608 West 22nd Street, Austin , TX 78705, phone (512) 476-5295, fax (512) 499-0889, *drives, memory up-grades, modems, accelerators.*

MacWarehouse, P.O. Box 3013, 1720 Oak Street, Lakewood, NJ 08701-3013, phone (800) 255-6227.
MacZone,17411 NE Union Hill Road, Redmond, WA 98052-6716, phone (800) 248-0800.

Mirror, 5498 West 76th Street, Edina, MN 55439, phone (800) 643-4143, fax (612) 832-0052, *systems and peripherals.*

PrePRESS Direct, 11 Mt. Pleasant Avenue, East Hanover, NJ, phone (800) 443-6600.

Relax Technology, 3101 Whipple Road, Union City, CA 94587, phone (510) 471-6112, fax (510) 471-6267, *peripherals.*

Syex Express,1030 Wirt Road, #400, Houston, TX 77055, phone (800) 876-3467, *systems and peripherals.*

Third Wave, 7301 Burnet Road Suite 102, Austin, TX 78757, phone (512) 477-9845, fax (512) 476-9241, *systems and peripherals.*

DATA

American Library Directory, R.R. Bowker Co. 245 West 17th Street, New York, NY 10011 **Lists all libraries and acquisition librarians.**

Ayer's Directory of Publishing, **Find sources for possible book reviews.** Available at large libraries.

Bacon's Publicity Checker, Bacon Information Services, 332 South Michigan Avenue, Chicago, IL 60604, phone (312) 922-2400. **Find sources for possible book reviews.** Available at large libraries.

Bacon's Radio and Television Directory, Bacon Information Services, 332 South Michigan Avenue, Chicago, IL 60604, phone (312) 922-2400. **Lists virtually every radio and television station in the country** Available at large libraries.

BOOKLIST, American Library Association, 50 Huron Street, Chicago, IL 60611. **Publishes periodical of book reviews especially for acquisition librarians.**

Copyright Basics, Register of Copyright, Library of Congress, Washington, DC 20559.

Creating Direct Mail Letters, Dartnell Corporation, 117 West Micheltorena, Santa Barbara, CA 93101-9978. **Loose leaf collection of outstanding direct mail letters.**

Directory of On-Line Databases Cuadra Associates, Inc. 11835 West Olympic Blvd., Suite 855, Los Angeles, CA 90064, phone (213) 478-0066 $95 per year.

Directory of Special Libraries and Information Centers, Available in bookstores. **Helps find specialized information valuable to publishers and developers of data bases.**

Encyclopedia of Associations, Gale Research Co. 835 Penobscot Building, Detroit, MI 48226, phone (313) 961-2241 Usually available in large libraries. **Lists almost all associations by classification and interests.**

Literary Marketplace, R.R. Bowker Co. 245 West 17th Street, New York, NY 10011 **Massive resource bank for writers' wishing to sell their work.**

The Newsletter Yearbook Directory, **Find sources for possible book reviews.** Available at large libraries.

The Red Book of Advertisers, National Register Publishing Co., Inc. 3004 Glenview Road, Wilmette, IL 60091, phone (312) 256-6067 **Lists major advertisers and their ad agencies. Good for ad sales solicitation.**

The Standard Periodical Directory, 3004 Glenview Road, Wilmette, IL 60091 **Find sources for possible book reviews.** Available at large libraries.

Standard Rate and Data Service, 3004 Glenview Road, Wilmette, IL 60091 **Publication supplies advertising rates and data on all major periodicals.** Available at large libraries.

Ulrich's International Periodical Directory, **Find sources for possible book reviews.** Available at large libraries.

Working Press of the Nation, **Find sources for possible book reviews.** Available at large libraries.

ELECTRONIC MAIL SERVICES
Dialcom E-Mail, Inc., 6120 Executive Blvd. Suite 500, Rockville, MD 20852, phone (301) 881-9020.

EasyLink, Western Union 1 Lake Street, Upper Saddle River, NJ 07054, phone (800) 527-5184,(201) 825-5000 .

EasyPlex/InfoPlex, CompuServe, Inc. 5000 Arlington Centre Blvd., Columbus, OH 43220, phone (614)457-8600.

MCI Mail, MCI Telecommunications Corp.,Inc. 200 M. Street, N.W., Washington, DC 20036, phone (800) 444-6245, (202) 293-4255.

Telemail, Telenet Communications Corp., 12490 Sunrise Valley Drive, Reston, VA 22096, phone (800) 336-0437, (703) 689-6300.

LOOSE LEAF BINDERS
American Thermoplastic Co., 622 Second Avenue, Pittsburgh, PA 15219-2086, phone (800) 456-6602, (412) 261-6657, fax (412) 642-7464, *consistently low prices.*

Dilley Manufacturing Company, 215 East Third Street, Des Moines, IA 50309, phone (800) 247-5087, (515) 288-7289, *full range of info-packaging products.*

LOW COST PROCESS COLOR PRINTERS (some are gang printers)
Ad Color, 149 Westchester Avenue, Port Chester, NY 10573, phone (914) 937-0005.

American Color Printing, 1731 N.W. 97 Avenue, Plantation, FL 33322, phone (305) 473-4392, fax (305) 473-8621.

Catalog King, 1 Entin Road, Clifton, NJ 07014, phone (800) 223-5751, (212) 695-0711.

Challenge Graphics, Inc., 18 Connor Lane, Deer Park, NY 11729, phone (800) 242-5364.

Direct Press/Modern Litho, 386 Oakwood Road, Huntington Station, NY 11746, phone (800) 347-3285, (516) 271-7000.

Econocolor, The Nielson Company, 7405 Industrial Road, Florence, KY 41042-2997, phone (606) 525-7405.

Express Color, 405 S.E. 80 Avenue, Portland, OR 97215-1527, phone (800) 388-8831, (503) 254-5537, fax (503) 255-4632, *not a gang printer but priced like one.*

Getz & McGrew Lithography Company, Inc., P.O. Box 15004, 14250 Santa Fe Trail Drive, Lenexa, KS 66285-5004, phone (800) 899-0707, (913) 599-0707, fax (913) 599-1946.

Hi-Tech Color House, 5901 North Cicero Avenue, Chicago, IL 60646, phone (800) 621-4004, (312) 588-8200.

Instant Web, 7951 Powers Blvd., Chanhassen, MN 55317, phone (612) 474-0961.

McGrew Color Graphics, 1615 Grand Avenue, Kansas City, MO 64108, phone (800) 877-7700, fax (816) 221-3154.

Mitchell Graphics, 2230 East Mitchell, Petoskey, MI 49770, phone (800) 841-6793, (616) 347-5650, fax (616) 347-9255.

Modern Graphic Arts, 3131 13th Avenue North, Saint Petersberg, FL 33713, phone (800) 237-8474, (813) 323-3131.

MultiPrint Company, 555 West Howard Street, Skokie, IL 60077, phone (800) 858-9999, (708) 677-7770, fax (708) 677-7544.

MWM Dexter, 107 Washington Street, Aurora, MO 65606, phone (800) 641-3398, (417) 678-2135, fax (417) 678-3626.

One Stop Printing, Inc., 9835 Max Shapiro Way, South El Monte, CA 91733, phone (818) 575-8688, fax (818) 579-3378.

Pinecliffe Printers, 1815 North Harrison Street, Shawnee, OK 74801, phone (405) 275-7351.

The Press, 18780 West 78th Street, Chanhassen, MN 55317, phone

(800) 336-2680, (612) 937-9764, *sheet fed and web.*
Rapidocolor, 101 Brandywine Parkway, West Chester, PA 19380,
phone (800) 872-7436, (215) 344-0500, fax (215) 344-0506, *sheet fed.*

Saltzman Printers/Combo Color, 50 Madison Street, Maywood, IL
60153-2399, phone (800) 952-2800, (312) 344-4500.

Service Web Offset, 2568 South Dearborn Street, Chicago, IL 60616,
phone (800) 621-1567, (312) 567-7000, *web press.*

Ultra-Color Corporation, 1814 Washington Avenue, Saint Louis, MO
63103, phone (314) 241-0300, *sheet fed.*

GENERAL
Standard Book Numbering Agency, R.R. Bowker Co. 245 West 17th
Street, New York, NY 10011 *Supplies ISBN number, required of most
books distributed through retail stores.*

LARGE FORMAT COLOR OUT-PUT
Digicolor, 1300 Dexter Avenue N, Seattle, WA 98109, phone (206)
284-2198, fax (206) 285-9664, *IRIS Ink Jet prints up to 33" x 46",
Versatec prints.*

Electronic Images, 430 First Avenue N, Suite 230, Minneapolis, MN
55401, phone (800) 441-2166, *IRIS Ink Jet prints up to 33" x 46",
DisplayMaker prints up to 36" x 110".*

Photo Lab, Inc., 1026 Redna Terrace, Cincinnatti, OH 45215, phone
(800) 452-4420.

Slide Service, Inc., Novachromes, 2537 25th Avenue South,
Minneapolis, MN 55406, phone (612) 721-2434, fax (612) 721-4855.

MAGAZINES
Aldus Magazine, P.O. Box 5448, Pittsfield, MA 01203-9315, *free to
registered Aldus customers.*

Color Publishing, P.O. Box 3184, Tulsa, OK 74101, *free to professionals.*

Current Books, P.O. Box 34468, Bethesda, MD 20827, *biannual ex-
cerpts new books and lists best sellers, useful to book publisher.*

Desktop Video World, P.O. Box 594, Mount Morris, IL 61054-7902,
useful if you are involved in video product production,VHS or CD.

Digital Imaging, 21150 Hawthorne Blvd., Torrance, CA 90503-9902,
free to professionals.

MacUser, P.O. Box 1688, Riverton, NJ 08077-9688.

Macworld, P.O. Box 51666, Boulder, CO 80321-1666.

Micro Publishing News, 21150 Hawthorne Blvd., Torrance, CA 90503-9902, *free to professionals, published by regions, ask if there is an edition in your region.*

Publish, P.O. Box 5039, Brentwood, TN 37024-9816, *interesting technically oriented publication.*

Small Press, Kymbolde Way, Wakefield, RI 02879-9910, *primarily concerned with literary and economic issues..*

Writer's Digest, P.O. Box 2124, Harlan IA 51593-2313, *worth a subscription for the ads.*

SLIDE IMAGING
Copy-CAD Imaging, Inc., phone (800) 866-2983, fax (312) 419-1390.

Show & Tell, 39 West 38th Street, New York, NY 10018, phone (212) 840-2912, fax (212) 840-7953, modem (212) 840-9464.

SlideImagers, 22 Seventh Street, Atlanta, GA 30308, phone (404) 873-5353.

STOCK COPY
PAGES Editorial Service, 300 North State Street, Chicago, IL 60610, (312) 222-9245 fax (312) 222-9637.

TRAINING
CareerTAPES Enterprises, P.O. Box 309 Center Harbor, NH 03226, phone (603) 253-7470 *Rent MacAcademy videos by mail.*

Comp-U-Learn, 621 Southwest Alder Street, Suite 700, Portland, OR 97205, *Computer training on video tapes.*

MacAcademy, 477 South Nova Road, Ormond Beach, FL 32174, phone (904) 677-1918.

ViaGrafix, phone (800) 842-4723, fax (918) 825-6744, *PageMaker training on video tapes.*

APPENDIX

In order to provide you with the most comprehensive manual possible, we have included six documents that have become vital to our publishing business;

1. a proposal/sales contract
2. a progress report
3. a request for quotation
4. a purchase order
5. a customer approval form
6. customer survey form

We also included a twelve page sample edition of *Profitable Promotions*, a newsletter published for clients and prospects. It is based on the principal that sharing useful information is one of the most effective ways to build client confidence and loyalty.

Also, the article "Create Stunning Color Promotions" will be useful to those who wish to concentrate on printing sales. It explains how your customers can save on color printing by creating their own simple mechanicals. Actually, you will be the big beneficiary of this article because people will bring you work to print that requires little attention, save a purchase order and postage to a gang printer. By eliminating the tedious layout-approval-revisions-approval process you can sell much more printing and operated on a s maller mark-up, thus benefiting your customers.

This technique will certainly not work with everyone. Many customers lack the focus and skill to produce a flyer or brochure. They will want your creative input and assurance that "their creation" will be an effective selling tool. Others with the need for multi-photo layouts or specialized copy and charts will also require personal attention. However a new prospect who opens their initial interview with the infamous statement; "We really don't have any (or much) money," is the perfect candidate to receive a reprint of this article. It is far better to let them do their own prep-work and make a modest mark-up on the printing than to spend hours with them only to find that you've exhausted their entire budget on consultation and design and there is nothing left for film, ink and paper.

We have also included an article for a publication directed to event and meeting planners. This is an example of a very effective promotional technique that you can use to establish yourself as an expert in your field. Hundreds of publications need interesting, well written copy every week. By supplying some of that copy you can establish credibility and name recognition for your firm at virtually no cost. You are also welcome to reproduce this article under your authorship with no additional copyright clearance.

We have included a price list, developed to give customers ballpark quotation on their projects.

Only these documents are available for copy or adaptation. All other sections of this book are covered by our copyright and no other section may be copied or excerpted for any purpose without the expressed consent of the copyright holder. Furthermore, we are neither attorneys or accountants and offer these documents purely as information. We take no responsibility for the results produced by the documents and strongly urge our readers to review all contracts they intend to sign with appropriate professionals.

THE PROPOSAL

During ten years of design practice we evolved the modular proposal system shown here. It is a synthesis of forms produced by several professional and trade organizations, but with an important addition. After reviewing the forms suggested by these organizations, most clients reacted as though they were being brutalized. The cold harsh "legalese" was not only confusing, it was intimidating. We have reversed this effect by using the proposal contract to inform our clients about the work we do, the way we charge for that work, even ways in which they can realize cost savings. Yes, there is still fine print, lots of it. It is necessary to protect us and convince the client that we are serious professionals. But, at least we've made an attempt to explain it.

We keep our proposals as short as possible. When a client asks for design only we omit the sections and terms that pertain to printing. When a client has composed film and wants only printing we omit the *designer terms*. The introduction always remains the same. It doesn't hurts to remind clients that you offer a range of services. For the same reason, we seldom edit the expense form under *Project Description*. We believe in using every opportunity to tell the world what marvelous thing we can do.

Many publishers have used data base programs like *FileMaker Pro* to construct their proposal forms. This sound like a great idea beca use the invoice and proposal are only a few keystrokes apart. The problem is they look dorkey. I have tried to construct an attractive proposal using this method and failed. If your client is looking for someone to organize his thoughts on an attractive page, your own proposal had better look good. Who cares if you can spew out 30 per hour if they look like the machinations of a chemistry professor. I use a page layout program to construct our proposals and spend the extra hours needed to make them look presentable.

I admit the database approach offers an important advantage to those who rely heavily on printing sales for their income. By offering a range of print quantities higher than the client's original request you can often increase your sale without saying a word. This technique is particularly powerful if you offer a "unit cost" for each quantity. When a client understands that they can have twice as many catalogs for half the unit price they frequently find ways to employ the over-run. FileMaker Pro is great for constructing this sort of table.

Finally, your client must sign your proposal. Their purchase order just won't do, even if it refers to the terms of your proposal. Purchase orders protect the buyer, contracts protect both parties and in most cases the designer/printer is taking the larger risk.

THE PROGRESS REPORT

We use this document as an addendum to the proposal on complex jobs such as catalogs. It is also useful when accepting a project with an unusually short time-frame. The form helps determine who is responsible for what and when. If you make it an integral part of your proposal you will probably be protected against claims that you did not produce the work in a timely manner (assuming that you did.) We also issue updated versions at regular intervals during the course of a long job. This keeps the client apprised of progress and allows them to make necessary arrangements with suppliers and mailing houses. It also provides a polite, non-judgemental prod to clients who are holding up their project through failure to deliver samples, copy or approval.

The progress report can also be useful as an addendum to a purchase order. Use it on projects that require unusual cooperation by subcontractors to meet a deadline. Issue purchase orders to service providers, service bureaus and printers as soon as the parameters of the job have been defined. Make the progress report an integral part of the order and explain that the order is valid only as long as the schedule is met. Naturally, unavoidable delays are inherent in almost projects. Therefore it is only fair to update your vendors as frequently as you do your clients. Many printers need to keep their presses running to show even a modest profit. When you fall behind schedule you must give them the opportunity to reschedule their press-time at least a week in advance. This courtesy is vital to maintain a relationship with many custom printers. Furthermore, You will frequently find innovative ways to save time and money if everyone knows how and when their contribution effects the overall project.

THE REQUEST FOR QUOTATION

Properly used, this form may prove to be your single largest source of income. The most effective way to use the RFQ is in a merge mail letter or database format. We prefer to organize our lists of printers by equipment type in MicroSoft Word. These are the categories that work best for us:

1. Instant Printers (up to 11" x 17")
2. Small Sheetfed 2 Color (up to 24" x 35")
3. Cold Web and Half Web (can print uncoated stock only)
4. Large Sheetfed 4 Color
5. Heatset Web Under Four Colors
6. Heatset Web four to Six Colors
7. Large Combination Printers

Many printers fit several categories and so they should appear on more than one list. You may also wish to separate local, out of state and off-shore printers. When the specifications of a printing job become clear you simply:

1. copy an existing merge letter in which you have already created this form,
2. type in the new specs,
3. merge it with the appropriate list,
4. fax or fax-broadcast (if you have a fax-modum) to the printers.

Frequently, you will want to ask for slight variations of format, binding, quantity or delivery (to the printer) techniques on a single job. This form performs that function beautifully. Simply step and repeat the specifications down the page. Make the alternate specifications in italics and tell the printer that the second (third, forth or fifth) set of specs represent alternates of the same job.

PURCHASE ORDER

Most designers operate "on account" with stat houses and service bureaus. They assign job numbers to each project which the vendor is expected to note on their invoice, thus allowing the designer to assign each expense to the correct project. This technique is safe enough when specifications are simple and costs are low. However, it can be a serious mistake to operate this way on large (over $100.00) or complex jobs. Vendors should be notified that no invoice for $100.00 or more will be paid without a valid purchase order and job description.

The staffs of print shops and service bureaus tend to be composed of very literally minded folk. The precision required of these jobs demands it. You must adapt to this mindset if you are to prosper in this profession. Write down every detail you expect in a job, draw pictures, attach laser roughs, if possible. In short, leave nothing to chance.

You will probably want to allow a photographer, illustrator, writer or designer a degree of creative liberty. A description that is too tight can have the reverse effect when dealing with creative individuals. Your description should still specify those items that are vital to decent reproduction, such as height to width of live matter. Copyright issues should also be addressed in a purchase order to creative freelancers. Our understanding of current copyright law is that unless you include the "work-for-hire" statement on your order you are purchasing only a specific use of the creation, the ownership of the copyright remains with the creator. This can come as a nasty shock when you reprint a clients catalog and your photographer wants additional payment for shots he took two years ago. Unless you're dealing with Richard Avadon or Saul Bellows, the work for hire should be a part of all creative orders and you should own the copyright on everything your publish.

CUSTOMER APPROVAL FORM

Never, never, never commit money (or your good credit which is the same thing) to advance a project until your client has a pproved the previous phase. In days of old we needed four approval points. The client was expected to ok copy prior to typesetting and layouts prior to photo shoots. In today's contracted production schedules the two important approval points are:

1. on the last laser rough, before composed film, and
2. on the Chromalin proof, before the printing is ordered.

Naturally, a competent designer/publisher keeps a client informed at all phases of a project, but these two are critical to avoid eating big expenses.

CUSTOMER SURVEY FORM

One of the biggest mistake publishers make is that deep sigh of relief they omit when a project is delivered from the printer and it looks good. The implication is that they are satisfied and the job is done. No mindset looses clients and ends careers faster. The job is done when the client has been satisfied and you have received final payment. We usually wait 24 hours from the drop off of th e client's copies, then call them to assess their level of satisfaction. Assuming this level is moderate to high, the call frequently leads to the next assignment. Letting a client know you are genuinely concerned about their interests, not just collecting the final payment, is one of the most effective ways to establish a long and profitable relationship.

We feel this process is so important that we carry it a step further. Twice a year we mail survey forms and ask our clients to rate our service. Because the form can be anonymous, clients will frequently say things you can't get them to say face to face. If you have been building a solid repour with your clients most responses will be no surprise. The few that do catch you off guard are worth their weight in gold because they offer insights to your business, your pricing policies and your competition's activities. Many publishers can unwittingly build a reputation they neither planned or desired, such as "Good But Expensive," "Creative But Too Slow," or "Cheep But Sloppy."

Careful analysis of the returns should help you plan your business strategy, show you your strengths and help you focus on those accounts to whom you can provide the greatest satisfaction.

PACIFIC
DESIGN GROUP

PROPOSAL

TO:	Mr. Martin Christman	**NUMBER:**	62394
	Sensational Events	**DATE:**	December 3, 1993
	P.O. Box 883003	**RE:**	Bairis Invitations
	San Francisco, 94188-3003	**FROM:**	Richard Nodine
FAX:	415-822-7398	**ENCLOSURES:**	
PHONE:	415-822-7218	**COPY:**	

INTRODUCTION

Thank you for your interest in our services and the opportunity to assist you with your project.

We represent communications specialists; writers, designers, illustrators, photographers, fabricators, technicians and printers who have years of experience in telling our client's stories in the most appealing, cost effective manner. We offer truly custom service to every client. Each project is carefully analyzed to determine the most dramatic and economical approach. We offer solutions based on each project's unique requirements and our 25+ years of print media experience.

How Projects Are Priced

Our production process is a joint effort between client, designer, writers and craftspersons. The process begins with our client interview. Because we have no preconceived formats, we let you do the talking. It is important that we gain an overview of your business, how it operates and how this specific project will impact your business. With this understanding can we give you the exact product you require and make recommendations for future business expanding projects.

After our interview, we prepare a proposal. Unless you have specified otherwise the proposal will cover:

1. Design and mechanical labor,
2. Generation of photography and/or illustrations,
3. Copy writing,
4. Typesetting and the preparation of films for the printer,
5. The selection and supervision of the correct contractors from make-ready to delivery of your product.

The preparation of printed material involves the creation of an organized description of your merchandise line or services. The act of committing a description of your business to the printed page frequently provokes re-thinking of old policies, procedures and merchandising practices. It will not be unusual if you wish to make revisions during the course of your project's preparation. Even with our vast experience in interpreting our client's need and desires, it is impossible to anticipate all possible revisions. Therefore, our proposals reflect our best estimate of the time and material required to accomplish the job you described in our initial interview, without revisions.

We always quantify each element of the proposal so you know in advance how much attention we believe each We will perform additional tasks, as requested, during the course of any project. These might include revisions to copy, additional page layouts, additional photos or illustrations or any service not specifically covered by this proposal. Additional services are billed at the following rates:

design and consultation	$75.00 per hour
mechanical, drafting, research	$45.00 per hour
photography	$600.00 per half day
photo stylist	$400.00 per day

Your best defenses against revision charges are *organization* and *quantification*:

1. Organize your project in outline form. Know the major points you want to cover and the percent of your project they should occupy. Determine exactly what merchandise you wish to feature and list the important selling points of each item.

2. Check the "Project Description" section of our proposal. Make sure it includes every aspect of the job you expect.

3. If possible, revisions should be made in the earlier stages of the project because they become more expensive as the job progresses.

Both Progress Statements and Estimates are issued to our clients periodically during the course of a project.

Our Brokerage Services Save You Time and Money
Proposals often include the cost of services and materials purchased from outside contractors and vendors. It is customary for these expenses to carry a modest markup. Because of our experience in acquiring these services our client's costs are usually far below what they might be if our clients were to shop for these services independently.

For the novice, print buying can be a complex and confusing chore. Virtually no printer will turn down a job. If your job doesn't fit his capacity he will either take it to another printer and charge you a mark-up or he will try to print it himself and risk producing a second-rate product. Over the years, we have developed a global data base of printers with every possible combination of specialities. Once we have established the parameters of your project, we comb our data base for the printer with the exact equipment and skills to produce you job at the lowest cost.

Our Policies are Governed by Industry Standards
The American Institute of Graphic Artist, The Graphic Artist Guild, the Graphic Arts Industries Association, the Graphic Arts Technical Foundation, the National Association of Printers and Lithographers and the Printing Industries of America all publish standard practices and terms. We have distilled the terms listed at the end of this contract from those of the organizations listed above. These terms and practices are time-tested standards of the industry. If you have any questions about them, or feel your project should be treated as an exception, please don't hesitate to discuss your concerns with us.

A10

Proofing Procedures

We make every effort to insure the correctness of your document. We use both computer spell checkers and grammar checkers to edit text We review and enhance photos with the latest digital programs. However, the final responsibility for proofing always lies with you, the client. You will receive at least two opportunities to proof your project. First, you will receive black and white laser prints of your job which must be approved before final film is generated. Second, you will receive color proofs (for full color projects) or blueline proofs (for spot color projects) which you must also approve before your project is printed. If time constraints make it impossible for you to perform either proofing process, you may elect to sign a standard waiver, allowing us to proceed.

Finally

Many of our clients bring us projects that require extensive research, planning, and development. Although we welcome this type of challenge, we must caution you that your best value is achieved when you know what you want to say and to whom you want to say it. Give us clear guide lines and we can give you the most economical job possible. We are always pleased to assist clients in the development of copy. But, if you prefer to write your own we can accept it in a variety of word processing programs in both IBM and Macintosh formats. You can achieve added savings by providing finished copy on disk.

PROJECT DESCRIPTION:

Create an eight page 5.5" x 8.5" saddle stitched "Passport" party invitations consisting of a full color cover on 10 pt. King James Cover and a two color insert on 60# Basketweve Security Stock. Print 600 copies and provide white wove stock booklet envelopes with black (only) return address.

Production Costs:

2	design hours	140.00	computer hours	0.0
	illustration fees	n.c.	scans	0.0
2	mechanical hours	90.00	film & processing	0.0
	photography hours	0.0	electronic imaging	0.0
	photo assistant hours	0.0	site costs	0.0
	styling hours	0.0	equipment/prop rental	0.0
	type/calligraphy fees	0.0	transportation	0.0
	image manipulation	0.0		

Printing Costs:

composite film & proof	133.00	line film	19.00
printing	625.00	die cutting	0.0
special stock	0.0	embossing	0.0
folding	60.00	scoring	0.0
trimming	0.0	perforation	0.0
special coating	0.0	hand finishing	0.0
thermography	0.0	mounting / lamination	0.0
stock envelopes	180.00	envelope conversion	0.0

SUBTOTAL	1247.00
TAX	105.99
SHIPPING	48.00
TOTAL	2596.92

A11

Thank you for the opportunity to be of service.

Designer's Terms: 1. A deposit of one third the gross amount of this contract is required to begin the project. A second payment of one third the gross amount is due upon acceptance of layouts and a third payment of one third the gross amount of this contract is due upon acceptance of the Chromlin proofs, prior to press run. A final invoice will be rendered upon delivery of the project at which time client will be charged or credited for any overage or shortage in the run. 1. Time for Payment. All invoices are payable within thirty (30) days of receipt. A one and one half percent monthly service charge is payable on all overdue balances. The grant of any license or right of copyright is conditioned on receipt of full payment. 2. Estimates. The fees and expenses shown are minimum estimates only. Final fees and expenses shall be shown when invoice is rendered. Client's approval shall be obtained for any increase in fees or expenses that exceed the original estimate by 10% or more. 3. Changes. Client shall be responsible for making additional payments for changes requested by Client in original assignment description. The Client shall offer the Designer the first opportunity to make any changes. 4. Expenses. Client shall reimburse Designer for all expenses arising from this assignment, including the payment of any sales tax due on this assignment and shall advance one third the total amount of this estimate to the Designer for payment of said expenses. 5. Cancellation. In the event of cancellation of this assignment, ownership of all copyrights and the original artwork is retained by the Designer and a cancellation fee for work completed, based on the contract price and expenses already incurred, shall be paid by the Client. 6. Ownership of Artwork. The Designer retains ownership of all original artwork, whether preliminary or final, and the Client shall return such artwork within thirty days of use. 8. Releases. Client will indemnify Designer against all claims and expenses, including reasonable attorney's fees, due to uses for which no release was requested in writing or for uses which exceed authority granted by a release. 9. Modifications. Modification of the agreement must be written, except that the invoice may include, and Client shall be obligated to pay, fees or expenses that were orally authorized in order to progress promptly with work. 10. Arbitration. Any disputes in excess of $2500.00 arising out of this Agreement shall be submitted to binding arbitration before the Joint Ethics Committee or a mutually agreed upon arbitrator pursuant to the rules of the American Arbitration Association. The Arbitrator's award shall be final and judgment may be entered upon it in any court having jurisdiction thereof. 11. Acceptance of Terms. The above terms incorporate Article 2 of the Uniform Commercial Code. If not objected to within ten (10) days, these terms shall be deemed acceptable. This proposal offering is valid and effective for thirty (30) days from the date hereon. Thereafter the offering must be reconfirmed by the designer.12. Code of Fair Practice. The Client and Designer agree to comply with the provisions of the Code of Fair Practice, a copy of which may be obtained from the Joint Ethics Committee, P.O. Box 179 Grand Central Station. New York, New York 10017.

Printers Terms: 1. Quotation. A quotation not accepted within thirty (30) days is subject to review. 2. Orders. Orders regularly entered, verbal or written, can not be cancelled except upon terms that will compensate printer against loss. 3. Experimental Work. Experimental work performed at customer's request, such as sketches, drawings, composition, plates, presswork and materials will be charged for at current rates and may be used without consent of the printer. 4. Preparatory Work. Sketches, copy, dummies and all preparatory work created or furnished by the printer, shall remain his exclusive property and no use of same shall be made, nor any ideas obtained therefrom be used, except upon compensation to be determined by the printer. 5. Condition of Copy. Estimates for typesetting are based on the receipt of original copy or manuscript clearly typed, double spaced on 8 1/2" .000000 11" uncoated stock, one side only. Condition of copy which deviates from this standard is subject to re-estimating and pricing review by printer at time of submission of copy, unless otherwise specified in estimate. 6. Preparatory Materials. Art work, type, plates negatives, positives and other items when supplied by the printer shall remain his exclusive property unless otherwise agreed in writing. 7. Alterations. Alterations represent work performed in addition to the original specifications. Such additional work shall be charged at current rates and be supported with documentation upon request. 8. Proofs. Proofs shall be submitted with original copy. Corrections are to be made on "master set," returned marked "OK" or "OK with corrections" and signed by customer. If revised proofs are desired, request must be made when proofs are returned. Printer regrets any errors that may occur through production undetected, but cannot be held responsible for errors if the work is printed per customer's OK, or if changes are communicated verbally. Printer shall not be responsible for errors if the customer has not ordered or has refused to accept proofs or has failed to return proofs with indication of changes or has instructed printer to proceed without submission of proofs. 9. Press Proofs. Unless specifically provided in printer's quotation, press proofs will be charged for at current rates. An inspection sheet of any form can be submitted for customer approval, at no charge, provided customer is available at the press during the time of makeready. Any changes, corrections or loss press time due to customer's change of mind or delay will be charged for at current rates. 10. Color Proofing. Because of differences in equipment, paper, inks and other conditions between color proofing and production pressroom operations, a reasonable variation in color between color proofs and completed job shall constitute acceptable delivery. Special inks and proofing stocks will be forwarded to customer's suppliers upon request at current rates. 11. Over-runs or Under-runs. Over runs or under runs not to exceed 10% on ordered up to 10,000 copies and/or the percentage agreed upon over or under quantities ordered above 10,000 copies shall constitute acceptable delivery. Printer will bill for actual quantity delivered within this tolerance. If customer requires guaranteed "no less than" delivery, percentage tolerance of overage must be doubled. 12. Customer Property. The printer will maintain fire, extended coverage, vandalism, malicious mischief and sprinkler leakage insurance on all property belonging to the customer, while such property is in the printer's possession; printer's liability for such property shall not exceed the amount recoverable from such insurance. 13. Delivery. Unless otherwise specified, the price quoted is for single shipment, without storage, F.O.B. local customer's place of business or F.O.B. printer's platform for out of town customers. Proposals are based on continuous and uninterrupted delivery of complete order, unless specified. Special priority pickup or delivery service will be provided at current rates upon customer's request. Materials delivered from customer or his suppliers are verified with delivery ticket as to cartons, packages or items shown only. The accuracy of quantities indicated on such tickets cannot be verified and printer cannot accept liability for such shortage based on supplier's tickets. The title for finished work shall pass to the customer upon delivery, to the carrier at shipping point or upon mailing of invoices for finished work, whichever occurs first. 14. Production Schedules. Production schedules will be established and adhered to by customer and printer, provided that neither shall incur any liability or penalty for delays due to state of war, riot, civil authority and acts of God or other causes beyond the control of customer or printer. 15. Customer Furnished Materials. Paper stock, camera copy, film, color separations and other customer furnished materials shall be manufactured, packed and delivered to printer's specifications. Additional cost due to delays or impaired production caused by specification deficiencies shall be charged to the customer. 16. Terms. Payment shall be net cash thirty (30) days from date of invoice unless otherwise provided in writing. Claims for defects, damages or shortages must be made by the customer in writing within a period of thirty (30) days after delivery. Failure to make such claim within the stated period shall constitute irrevocable acceptance and an admission that they fully comply with terms, conditions and specifications. Printer's liability shall be limited to stated selling price of any defective goods, and shall in no event include special or consequential damages, including profits (or profit lost). As security for payment of any sum due or to become due under terms of any Agreement, printer shall have the right, if necessary, to retain possession of and shall have a lien on all customer property in printer's possession including work in progress and finished work. 17. Indemnification. The customer shall indemnify and hold harmless the printer from any and all loss, cost, expense and damages on account of any and all manner of claims, demands, actions and proceedings that may be instituted against the printer on grounds alleging that the said printing violates any copyright or any proprietary right of any person, or that it contains any matter that is libelous or scandalous, or invades any person's right to privacy or other personal rights, except to the extent that the printer has contributed to the matter. The customer agrees to, at the customers own expense, promptly defend and continue the defense of any such claim, demand, action or proceeding that may be brought against the printer, provided that the printer shall promptly notify the customer with respect thereto, and provide further that the printer shall give to the customer such reasonable time as the exigencies of the situation may permit in which to undertake and continue the defense thereof.

_____   _____

accepted and approved for Pacific Design Group   date

_____   _____

accepted and approved for Sensational Events   date

A12

PACIFIC
DESIGN GROUP

PROGRESS REPORT

TO:	Mr. Charles Martin	**NUMBER:**	101177
	Mr. Keven Martin	**DATE:**	February 4, 1992
	Denver Barral Co.	**RE:**	Safety Catalog
	161 Erie Street	**FROM:**	Richard Nodine
	San Francisco, CA 94103	**ENCLOSURES:**	
FAX:	864-0912	**COPY:**	
PHONE:	241-8350		

As a service to our customers we provide periodic progress reports on all complex projects. This is neither an invoice nor statement but because it describes over-runs in cost or time not covered by our original proposal, we would like you to review it and confirm that you are in agreement by returning a signed a copy (a fax will be fine).

Thank you for your consideration.

ORIGINAL PROJECT DESCRIPTION:
Create a new 16 page, 8.5" x 11", saddle stitched, full color book illustrating the Denver Barral Co. line of safety items to be printed on 80# coated text with selfcover.

photography (2 days)	2400.00	1 model (2 hours)	140.00
film & processing	320.00	copy	N.C.
design	1120.00	mechanicals	280.00
typography	1164.80	film separations	2769.00
printing (10000 copies)	6448.00	air freight for 2500 copies	290.00
		SUBTOTAL	14931.80
		TAX	1244.55
		TOTAL	15886.35

DA Y	DATE	PLANNED ACTIVITY	BY	ACTUAL ACTIVITY
1	10/19 M	INITIAL MEETING	K D B C	OK
		PREPARE FINAL PROPOSAL	D	OK
2	10/20 T	DELIVER MERCHANDISE	K	OK
		SUBMIT PAGINATION OUTLINE	K	OK
3	10/21 W	SUBMIT ANNOTATED COPY	K	OK
4	10/22 Th	DEVELOP PROTOTYPE LAYOUTS, 2 PGS	D	OK
		DEVELOP INITIAL COPY	B D	OK
5	10/23 F	DEVELOP PROTOTYPE LAYOUTS, 2 PGS	D	OK
		DEVELOP INITIAL COPY	B D	OK
6	10/24 S	DEVELOP PROTOTYPE LAYOUTS, 2 PGS	D	OK
		DEVELOP INITIAL COPY	B D	OK
7	10/25 Su			
8	10/26 M	DEVELOP PROTOTYPE LAYOUTS, 2 PGS	D B	OK
		DEVELOP INITIAL COPY	B D	OK
9	10/27 T	DEVELOP PROTOTYPE LAYOUTS, 2 PGS	D B	OK
		DEVELOP INITIAL COPY	B D	OK
10	10/28 W	SUBMIT PROTOTYPE LAYOUT	D B	OK
		REVIEW PROTOTYPE LAYOUT	K C	OK
11	10/29 Th	REVIEW PROTOTYPE LAYOUT	K C	OK
12	10/30 F	REVIEW PROTOTYPE LAYOUT	K C	OK
		MEETING ON PROTOTYPE LAYOUT	K C B D	CLIENT REQUESTED PROTOTYPE LAYOUT REVISIONS
13	10/31S	DEVELOP ALL LAYOUTS & COPY	D B	REVISIONS *
		KEVEN TRAVELING		REVISIONS *
14	11/01 Su	DEVELOP ALL LAYOUTS & COPY	D B	OK
		KEVEN TRAVELING		
15	11/02 M	DEVELOP ALL LAYOUTS & COPY	D B	OK
		KEVEN TRAVELING		OK
16	11/03 T	DEVELOP ALL LAYOUTS & COPY	D B	OK
		KEVEN TRAVELING		OK
17	11/04 W	PRESENT ALL LAYOUTS & COPY	D B	OK FAX LAYOUTS TO ORLANDO
		KEVEN RETURNS		
18	11/05 Th	REVIEW LAYOUTS	K C	
		MEETING ON ALL LAYOUTS	K C B D	
19	11/06 F	REVIEW LAYOUTS	K C	OK / CLIENTS REQUEST SUBSTANTIAL REVISIONS
20	11/07 S	FINAL PHOTOGRAPHY	D	REVISIONS *
		KEVEN TRAVELING		
21	11/08 Su	FINAL PHOTOGRAPHY	D	REVISIONS *
		KEVEN TRAVELING		
22	11/09 M	FINAL PHOTOGRAPHY	D	REVISIONS *
		KEVEN TRAVELING		
23	11/10 T	COMPOSE FILM	H K	REVISIONS *
		KEVEN TRAVELING		
24	11/11 W	COMPOSE FILM	H K	REVISIONS * / SUBMITTED PARTIAL REVISIONS, CLIENT REQUESTED FURTHER REVISIONS
25	11/12 Th	COMPOSE FILM	H K	REVISIONS *

DAY	DATE	PLANNED ACTIVITY	BY	ACTUAL ACTIVITY
26	11/13 F	COMPOSE FILM	HK	REVISIONS * / FIRST PROGRESS REPORT
29	11/16 M	COMPOSE FILM	HK	DESIGN COVER
		KEVEN TRAVELING		
30	11/17 T	COMPOSE FILM	HK	DESIGN COVER / REVISIONS*
		KEVEN TRAVELING		
31	11/18 W	COMPOSE FILM	HK	
		KEVEN TRAVELING		
32	11/19 Th	COMPOSE FILM	HK	MEET WITH CHRISTOPHE DISCUS FURTHER REVISIONS / WRITE COPY (NO CHARGE)
		KEVEN TRAVELING		
33	11/20 F	COMPOSE FILM	HK	WRITE COPY (NO CHARGE) / REVISIONS*
		KEVEN TRAVELING		
34	11/21 S	KEVEN TRAVELING		
35	11/22 Su	KEVEN RETURNS		
36	11/23 M	COMPOSE FILM	HK	DELIVER COMPLETE B&W PROOFS WITH COPY
37	11/24 T	COMPOSE FILM	HK	DELIVER 2 COLOR PROOFS*
38	11/25 W	RUN PRESS PROOFS	HK	DENVER REVIEWS PROOFS
39	11/26 Th	PRESS PROOFS LEAVE HONG KONG		DENVER REVIEWS PROOFS
40	11/27 F	SUBMIT COLOR PROOFS	B D	DENVER REVIEWS PROOFS
41	11/28 S	REVIEW PROOFS	K C	DENVER REVIEWS PROOFS
42	11/29 Su	REVIEW PROOFS	K C	DENVER REVIEWS PROOFS
43	11/30 M	INDICATE CHANGES	D B	DENVER REVIEWS PROOFS
44	12/01 T	MAKE CHANGES	HK	DENVER REVIEWS PROOFS
45	12/02 W	MAKE CHANGES	HK	DENVER REVIEWS PROOFS
46	12/03 Th	MAKE CHANGES	HK	MEETING WITH KEN, ADDITIONAL CHANGES*
47	12/04 F	POSSIBLE SECOND PROOFS	HK	MAKE ADDITIONAL CHANGES*
48	12/05 S			
49	12/06 Su			
50	12/07 M	APPROVE COLOR PROOFS	K C	MAKE ADDITIONAL CHANGES *
51	12/08 T			MAKE ADDITIONAL CHANGES *
52	12/09 W	PRINT BOOK	HK	DELIVER NEW PROOFS
53	12/10 Th	PRINT BOOK	HK	DENVER REVIEWS PROOFS / HOLD FOR APPROVAL
54	12/11 F	PRINT BOOK	HK	DENVER REVIEWS PROOFS / HOLD FOR APPROVAL
55	12/12 S			
56	12/13 Su			
57	12/14 M	PRINT BOOK	HK	
58	12/15 T	PRINT BOOK	HK	
59	12/16 W	PRINT BOOK	HK	
60	12/17 Th	PRINT BOOK	HK	Denver brings revisions and corrections
61	12/18 F	PRINT BOOK	HK	
62	12/19 S			
63	12/20 Su			

DAY	DATE	PLANNED ACTIVITY	BY	ACTUAL ACTIVITY
71	12/28			
72	12/29			
73	12/30			
74	12/31			
75	01/01			
76	01/02		PPM	reshoot
77	01/03			
78	01/04			
79	01/05		PPM	copy revisions & corrections *
80	01/06		PPM	copy revisions & corrections *
81	01/07			
82	01/08			
83	01/09			
84	01/10			
85	01/11			
86	01/12			
87	01/13		Doublet	submits revisions - revisions complete
88	01/14			
89	01/15			
90	01/16			
91	01/17			
92	01/18			
93	01/19			
94	01/20		PPM	shoot Christophe and windcone
95	01/21			
96	01/22		PPM	submit photos for approval
97	01/23			
98	01/24			
99	01/25			
100	01/26			
101	01/27		DENVER	submits photo revisions & corrections & copy revisions
102	01/28		PPM	make revisions & corrections *
103	01/29			
104	01/30			
105	01/31			
106	02/01			
107	02/02			
108	02/03			
109	02/04			
110	02/05		PPM	reshoot photos *
111	02/06			
112	02/07			
113	02/08	approves all layouts and photos	DENVER	

DAY	DATE	PLANNED ACTIVITY	BY	ACTUAL ACTIVITY
114	02/09	Lino out-put	PPM	
115	02/10	mechanical for 2 spreads	PPM	
116	02/11	send first mechanical to HK for proofs	PPM	
117	02/12			
118	02/13			
119	02/14			
120	02/15	begins color seps	HK	
121	02/16			
122	02/17			
123	02/18			
124	02/19			
125	02/20			
126	02/21			
127	02/22			
128	02/23			
129	02/24			
130	02/25			
131	02/26	delivers press proofs	HK	
132	02/27			
133	02/28			
134	03/01	receive proof and send to DENVER for approval	PPM	
135	03/02	if approved, prepare additional mechanicals		PPM
136	03/03			
137	03/04			
138	03/05			
139	03/06			
140	03/07	send mechanicals to HK	PPM	
141	03/08	receives mechanical and prepares film	HK	
142	03/09			
143	03/10			
144	03/11			
145	03/12			
146	03/13			
147	03/14			
148	03/15			
149	03/16			
150	03/17			
151	03/18			
152	03/19			
153	03/20			
154	03/21			
155	03/22			
156	03/23			
157	03/24			
158	03/25			

A17

159	03/26	sends press proof	HK
160	03/27		
161	03/28		

DAY	DATE	PLANNED ACTIVITY	BY	ACTUAL ACTIVITY
162	03/29	receives proof & sends to DENVER for approval	PPM	
163	03/30	begin printing if no changes	HK	
164	03/31			
165	04/01			
166	04/02			
167	04/03			
168	04/04			
169	04/05			
170	04/06			
171	04/07	sends 3000 by air	HK	
172	04/08	ships balance	HK	
	04/30	balance of order docks Oakland		
	04/31	messenger to Doublet		

* INDICATES UNBUDGETED EXPENSE

PROJECT DESCRIPTION to December 12, 1992:

In the interest of developing highly structured prototype we devoted extensive unbillable hours to the initial rough. Client made substantial changes in merchandise configuration and text format which required 25 hours of revision. most of this time was consumed by tedious type-fitting to make it possible to generate multiple versions (price) will little additional effort. Additional revisions requested during a two hour meeting on 12/3/92 required another10 hours revisions. Both sets of revisions are detailed in separate memos.

We developed costs on split-runs allowing two price changes within the 10,000 unit press-run. Client has not yet accepted this proposal.

photography (2 days)	2400.00	1 model (2 hours)	140.00
film & processing	320.00	copy	N.C.
73 design hours (16 billable)	1120.00	mechanicals	280.00
typography	1164.80	film separations	2769.00
printing (10000 copies)	6448.00	air freight for 2500 copies	290.00
35 revisions hours	2450.00	color prints	40.00
fax time to Orlando	5.68		
		SUBTOTAL	17427.48

PROJECT DESCRIPTION to January 4, 1993:

By agreement with the client PPM will absorb 10 hours of revisions.

photography (2 days)	2400.00	1 model (2 hours)	140.00
film & processing	320.00	copy N.C.	
73 design hours (16 billable)	1120.00	mechanicals	

PROJECT DESCRIPTION to February 4, 1993:
Client submitted revisions to copy which were accomplished. No time was billed for corrections. Client also requires reshoot or additional photos of vests (301, 931, 749 custom and 222) plus reshoot of coveralls, flags (7323, 7106, 7136, 7223, 7110, 7075, 7600, 7302, 7303) and plastic flagging. The cost of this reshoot will be reflected in subsequent reports.

photography (3 days)	3600.00	1 model (3 hours)	210.00
film & processing	320.00	copy N.C.	
73 design hours (16 billable)	1120.00	mechanicals	280.00
typography	1164.80	film separations	2769.00*
printing (10000 copies)	6448.00*	air freight for 2500 copies	290.00
38 revisions hours	2660.00	color prints	40.00
fax time to Orlando	5.68		
		SUBTOTAL	18417.48

Acknowledged by_____date_____

A19

PACIFIC
DESIGN GROUP

INVOICE

TO:	Mr. Martin Christman	**NUMBER:**	62394
	Sensational Events	**DATE:**	December 31, 1993
	P.O. Box 883003	**RE:**	Bairis Invitations
	San Francisco, 94188-3003	**TERMS:**	see reverse
		ENCLOSURES:	
FAX:	415-822-7398		
PHONE:	415-822-7218	**PROJECT:**	623
		P.O. #:	S02145

PROJECT DESCRIPTION:

Create an eight page 5.5" x 8.5" saddle stitched "Passport" party invitations consisting of a full color cover on 10 pt. King James Cover and a two color insert on 60# Basketweve Security Stock. Print 600 copies and provide white wove stock booklet envelopes with black (only) return address.

Production Costs:

2	design hours	140.00	computer hours	0.0
	illustration fees	n.c.	scans	0.0
2	mechanical hours	90.00	film & processing	0.0
	photography hours	0.0	electronic imaging	0.0
	photo assistant hours	0.0	site costs	0.0
	styling hours	0.0	equipment/prop rental	0.0
	type/calligraphy fees	0.0	transportation	0.0
	image manipulation	0.0		

Printing Costs:

composite film & proof	133.00	line film	19.00
printing	625.00	die cutting	0.0
special stock	0.0	embossing	0.0
folding	60.00	scoring	0.0
trimming	0.0	perforation	0.0
special coating	0.0	hand finishing	0.0
thermography	0.0	mounting / lamination	0.0
stock envelopes	180.00	envelope conversion	0.0

SUBTOTAL	1247.00
TAX	105.99
SHIPPING	48.00
TOTAL	2596.92

Thank you for the opportunity to be of service.

A20

TERMS

Designer's Terms: 1. A deposit of one third the gross amount of this contract is required to begin the project. A second payment of one third the gross amount is due upon acceptance of layouts and a third payment of one third the gross amount of this contract is due upon acceptance of the Chromlin proofs, prior to press run. A final invoice will be rendered upon delivery of the project at which time client will be charged or credited for any overage or shortage in the run. 1. Time for Payment. All invoices are payable within thirty (30) days of receipt. A one and one half percent monthly service charge is payable on all overdue balances. The grant of any license or right of copyright is conditioned on receipt of full payment. 2. Estimates. The fees and expenses shown are minimum estimates only. Final fees and expenses shall be shown when invoice is rendered. Client's approval shall be obtained for any increase in fees or expenses that exceed the original estimate by 10% or more. 3. Changes. Client shall be responsible for making additional payments for changes requested by Client in original assignment description. The Client shall offer the Designer the first opportunity to make any changes. 4. Expenses. Client shall reimburse Designer for all expenses arising from this assignment, including the payment of any sales tax due on this assignment and shall advance one third the total amount of this estimate to the Designer for payment of said expenses. 5. Cancellation. In the event of cancellation of this assignment, ownership of all copyrights and the original artwork is retained by the Designer and a cancellation fee for work completed, based on the contract price and expenses already incurred, shall be paid by the Client. 6. Ownership of Artwork. The Designer retains ownership of all original artwork, whether preliminary or final, and the Client shall return such artwork within thirty days of use. 8. Releases. Client will indemnify Designer against all claims and expenses, including reasonable attorney's fees, due to uses for which no release was requested in writing or for uses which exceed authority granted by a release. 9. Modifications. Modification of the agreement must be written, except that the invoice may include, and Client shall be obligated to pay, fees or expenses that were orally authorized in order to progress promptly with work. 10. Arbitration. Any disputes in excess of $2500.00 arising out of this Agreement shall be submitted to binding arbitration before the Joint Ethics Committee or a mutually agreed upon arbitrator pursuant to the rules of the American Arbitration Association. The Arbitrator's award shall be final and judgment may be entered upon it in any court having jurisdiction thereof. 11. Acceptance of Terms. The above terms incorporate Article 2 of the Uniform Commercial Code. If not objected to within ten (10) days, these terms shall be deemed acceptable. This proposal offering is valid and effective for thirty (30) days from the date hereon. Thereafter the offering must be reconfirmed by the designer.12. Code of Fair Practice. The Client and Designer agree to comply with the provisions of the Code of Fair Practice, a copy of which may be obtained from the Joint Ethics Committee, P.O. Box 179 Grand Central Station. New York, New York 10017.

Printers Terms: 1. Quotation. A quotation not accepted within thirty (30) days is subject to review. 2. Orders. Orders regularly entered, verbal or written, can not be cancelled except upon terms that will compensate printer against loss. 3. Experimental Work. Experimental work performed at customer's request, such as sketches, drawings, composition, plates, presswork and materials will be charged for at current rates and may be used without consent of the printer. 4. Preparatory Work. Sketches, copy, dummies and all preparatory work created or furnished by the printer, shall remain his exclusive property and no use of same shall be made, nor any ideas obtained therefrom be used, except upon compensation to be determined by the printer. 5. Condition of Copy. Estimates for typesetting are based on the receipt of original copy or manuscript clearly typed, double spaced on 8 1/2" .000000 11" uncoated stock, one side only. Condition of copy which deviates from this standard is subject to re-estimating and pricing review by printer at time of submission of copy, unless otherwise specified in estimate. 6. Preparatory Materials. Art work, type, plates negatives, positives and other items when supplied by the printer shall remain his exclusive property unless otherwise agreed in writing. 7. Alterations. Alterations represent work performed in addition to the original specifications. Such additional work shall be charged at current rates and be supported with documentation upon request. 8. Proofs. Proofs shall be submitted with original copy. Corrections are to be made on "master set," returned marked "OK" or "OK with corrections" and signed by customer. If revised proofs are desired, request must be made when proofs are returned. Printer regrets any errors that may occur through production undetected, but cannot be held responsible for errors if the work is printed per customer's OK, or if changes are communicated verbally. Printer shall not be responsible for errors if the customer has not ordered or has refused to accept proofs or has failed to return proofs with indication of changes or has instructed printer to proceed without submission of proofs. 9. Press Proofs. Unless specifically provided in printer's quotation, press proofs will be charged for at current rates. An inspection sheet of any form can be submitted for customer approval, at no charge, provided customer is available at the press during the time of makeready. Any changes, corrections or loss press time due to customer's change of mind or delay will be charged for at current rates. 10. Color Proofing. Because of differences in equipment, paper, inks and other conditions between color proofing and production pressroom operations, a reasonable variation in color between color proofs and completed job shall constitute acceptable delivery. Special inks and proofing stocks will be forwarded to customer's suppliers upon request at current rates. 11. Over-runs or Under-runs. Over runs or under runs not to exceed 10% on ordered up to 10,000 copies and/or the percentage agreed upon over or under quantities ordered above 10,000 copies shall constitute acceptable delivery. Printer will bill for actual quantity delivered within this tolerance. If customer requires guaranteed "no less than" delivery, percentage tolerance of overage must be doubled. 12. Customer Property. The printer will maintain fire, extended coverage, vandalism, malicious mischief and sprinkler leakage insurance on all property belonging to the customer, while such property is in the printer's possession; printer's liability for such property shall not exceed the amount recoverable from such insurance. 13. Delivery. Unless otherwise specified, the price quoted is for single shipment, without storage, F.O.B. local customer's place of business or F.O.B. printer's platform for out of town customers. Proposals are based on continuous and uninterrupted delivery of complete order, unless specified. Special priority pickup or delivery service will be provided at current rates upon customer's request. Materials delivered from customer or his suppliers are verified with delivery ticket as to cartons, packages or items shown only. The accuracy of quantities indicated on such tickets cannot be verified and printer cannot accept liability for such shortage based on supplier's tickets. The title for finished work shall pass to the customer upon delivery, to the carrier at shipping point or upon mailing of invoices for finished work, whichever occurs first. 14. Production Schedules. Production schedules will be established and adhered to by customer and printer, provided that neither shall incur any liability or penalty for delays due to state of war, riot, civil authority and acts of God or other causes beyond the control of customer or printer. 15. Customer Furnished Materials. Paper stock, camera copy, film, color separations and other customer furnished materials shall be manufactured, packed and delivered to printer's specifications. Additional cost due to delays or impaired production caused by specification deficiencies shall be charged to the customer. 16. Terms. Payment shall be net cash thirty (30) days from date of invoice unless otherwise provided in writing. Claims for defects, damages or shortages must be made by the customer in writing within a period of thirty (30) days after delivery. Failure to make such claim within the stated period shall constitute irrevocable acceptance and an admission that they fully comply with terms, conditions and specifications. Printer's liability shall be limited to stated selling price of any defective goods, and shall in no event include special or consequential damages, including profits (or profit lost). As security for payment of any sum due or to become due under terms of any Agreement, printer shall have the right, if necessary, to retain possession of and shall have a lien on all customer property in printer's possession including work in progress and finished work. 17. Indemnification. The customer shall indemnify and hold harmless the printer from any and all loss, cost, expense and damages on account of any and all manner of claims, demands, actions and proceedings that may be instituted against the printer on grounds alleging that the said printing violates any copyright or any proprietary right of any person, or that it contains any matter that is libelous or scandalous, or invades any person's right to privacy or other personal rights, except to the extent that the printer has contributed to the matter. The customer agrees to, at the customers own expense, promptly defend and continue the defense of any such claim, demand, action or proceeding that may be brought against the printer, provided that the printer shall promptly notify the customer with respect thereto, and provide further that the printer shall give to the customer such reasonable time as the exigencies of the situation may permit in which to undertake and continue the defense thereof.

PACIFIC
DESIGN GROUP

REQUEST FOR QUOTE

DATE:	10/11/93	**NUMBER:**	841
TO:	Mr. Tom Benedict	**RE:**	CR
	R.R. Donnelley	**FROM:**	Richard Nodine
	2000 Powell Street	**ENCLOSURES:**	
	Oakland, CA 94608	**COPY:**	
FAX:	510-658-0582		

We would appreciate receiving your quotation on the following job on or before Friday, October 15.

SPECIFICATIONS:		QUANTITY:	20000
title	Perspectives '93	total pages	24
trim size	8.5" x 5.5"	due date	open
text paper	70# offset	text ink	black & red
text screens	provided	text bleeds	three sides
text heavy reverses	20%	text halftones	24 provided in film
delivered to printer as	plate ready film	delivered on	10/17/93
cover stock	self	cover ink	black & red
cover heavy reverses	100% coverage outside	cover bleeds	4 sides outside
delivered to printer as	plate ready film	delivered on	10/17/93
binding	saddle stitched	packing	bulk

special instructions: Unlike conventional small books, this book stitches on the 5.5" side.

SPECIFICATIONS:		QUANTITY:	20000
title	Perspectives '93	total pages	24
trim size	5.5" x 8 1/2"	due date	open
text paper	70# offset	text ink	black & red
text screens	provided	text bleeds	three sides
text heavy reverses	20%	text halftones	24 provided in film
delivered to printer as	plate ready film	delivered on	10/17/93
cover stock	self	cover ink	black & red
cover heavy reverses	100% coverage outside	cover bleeds	4 sides outside
delivered to printer as	plate ready film	delivered on	10/17/93
binding	saddle stitched	packing	bulk

special instructions:

PACIFIC
D E S I G N   G R O U P

RELEASE TO GENERATE FILM

DATE: 7/15/93
TO: Mr. Lawrence Dalton
California Film Archives
146 Ninth Street
San Francisco, CA 94103
FAX: 621-6522

NUMBER: 800
RE: Library of American Cinema
FROM: Richard Nodine
ENCLOSURES: 0
COPY:

For your approval, we are attaching a black and white proof of the project noted above. Please review it and indicate your approval prior to film generation.

To avoid delay, please return the proof with this form. Thank you for your speedy response.

I have reviewed the attached document for correctness. Please generate film;

☐ without revisions

☐ with the following changes:

_____
_____
_____
_____

_____   _____
approved by   date

A23

PACIFIC
DESIGN GROUP

RELEASE TO PRINT

DATE:	7/30/93	**NUMBER:**	800
TO:	Mr. Lawrence Dalton	**RE:**	Library of American Cinema
	California Film Archives	**FROM:**	Richard Nodine
	146 Ninth Street	**ENCLOSURES:**	0
	San Francisco, CA 94103	**COPY:**	
FAX:	621-6522		

For your approval, we are attaching a color match proof of the project noted above. Please review it and indicate your approval prior to printing.

To avoid delay, please return the proof with this form. Thank you for your speedy response.

I have reviewed the attached document for correctness. Please print;

☐ without revisions

☐ with the following changes:

_____
_____
_____
_____

☐ Please generate new proofs for pages with revisions *(requires added time and restimation).*

☐ I accept revisions without additional proofs, go direct to print.

_____   _____
approved by   date

A24

PACIFIC
DESIGN GROUP

Please rate us on the following points:

	outstanding	very good	good	satisfactory	unsatisfactory
Assignments are completed on time.					
Assignments are completed accurately.					
Art style is appropriate to each assignment.					
Writing style is appropriate to each assignment.					
Design adds dimension and value to each assignment.					
Photography is sharp , well styled and appropriate.					
I am advised of the progress of assignments regularly.					
My instructions are followed precisely.					
Revisions are handled quickly.					
Most advanced technology is used for greatest efficiency.					
Printing quality					
Xerox quality					

Compared to other services in this market;

	low	average	high
Your creative service costs are			
Your production service costs are			
Your printing service costs are			

How could we serve you better?

_____

_____

_____

_____

_____

_____

_____

A25

PACIFIC
DESIGN GROUP

PURCHASE ORDER

TO: Mr. Jim Clemins
Paledin Press
2186 Third Street
San Francisco, CA 94110
FAX: 252-7376

JOB NUMBER: Program Insert
DATE: January 7, 1994
P.O. NUMBER 00347527
FROM: Richard Nodine
DELIVERY REQUIRED: January 8
CANCELLATION DATE: January 9

SHIP TO: Destination One Tent
Pier 32
San Francisco

ENCLOSURES:
3 film negatives
1 mock-up

VIA: your own

Please provide the following:

2000   two sided, black and one PMS cards from enclosed films
on 80# white bristol vellum. Background prints PMS 466.
Copy prints black.

         280.00

SUBTOTAL   280.00
TAX   resale
TOTAL   280.00

SPECIAL INSTRUCTIONS: please make sure the top and bottom of each side is
facing the same edge INVOICE MUST COME TO THIS OFFICE - NOT BE LEFT
WITH THE JOB

authorized by

PACIFIC
DESIGN GROUP

Create Stunning Full Color Promotions

It's easy to create beautiful postcards, brochures, catalog sheets and posters when you work with the experts at Pacific Print Media. We'll use our years of experience to insure that your printed piece dramatizes your product or service in the most cost effective way possible. The following are some useful hints to help you get the most from our service.

1. Always start with sharply focused, well-lighted photography. Snap-shots taken with low quality cameras in poor light conditions will never reproduce satisfactorily. If you send us photos that will not produce an adequate end-result we will return the job. We would rather loose one order than print the job and loose your good will.

A. Use the largest format photograph you can. The very best results will be obtained by using professional transparency film in the 4" x 5" format. The 2$1/4$" format is second best and 35 mm film is the smallest acceptable. The larger the photo will appear in your final print, the more important it is to use large original film. If you wish to enlarge a <u>small part</u> of your photo to full page size your final image will be less sharp than it appears in your original. Although we can work from prints, the color rendition is less vivid. If brilliant color is important to your product, use transparency film.

2. Purchase a pad of tracing or transparent layout paper from your art supply store to create your rough layout. Carefully draw a box the size of the page you are ordering in the center of the sheet. Use a t-square, triangle or another sheet of paper to ensure that your drawing is square to the page (figure A).

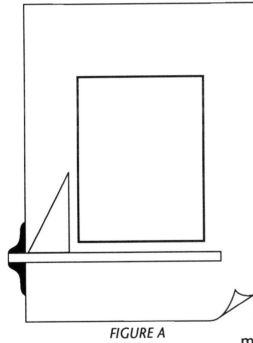

FIGURE A

A. To proportion your photo to your layout place another sheet of tracing paper over a print of your primary photo. Tape the tissue firmly in place. If you are working with a transparency you will want to have a Cannon or Xerox color print made to a convenient size. Most towns have service bureaus or quick printers that offer this service. Carefully draw a square box around the area of your photo you wish to print. Draw a diagonal line that touches opposite corners of the picture box (figure B).Trace the box and diagonal line in the corner of your layout. Using a t-square, triangle or another sheet of paper as a guide, you may enlarge your photo box to the size of your page, or any size in between. Just be sure the corners of your photo always intersect the diagonal line (figure C).

B. You may center your photo, print it off-center or make it bleed off the page. However, if you want to make your photo bleed, you must be sure it contains about 5% more image on each bleed edge than you want to see in the final print. Our printer will actually print more of the photo than you indicate and trim off the excess.

C. Place a number 1 on the back of the print of your primary photo and a number 1 in the corresponding picture box on your layout.

3. Locate the size and position of any additional photos on your page in the same way. Additional photos may be placed outside the primary photo or inset on the primary photo. If you opt to use an inset photo you should indicate a small boarder between the two photos to make the images more distinct (figure D).

A. Place a number 2 on the back of the print of your first additional photo and a number 2 in the corresponding picture box on your layout. Use additional numbers for subsequent photos.

4. Create a dramatic headline stressing customer benefits and indicate it's size and position on your layout. Headlines may be

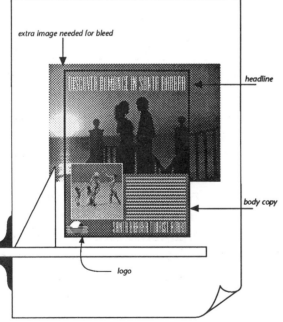

extra image needed for bleed

headline

body copy

logo

FIGURE C

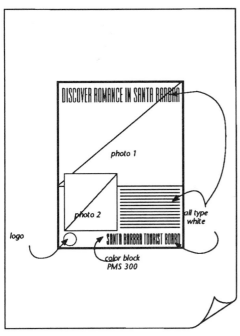

Your final layout should look like this.
FIGURE D

printed in black over a light area of your photo or in white over a dark area of your photo. If your photo has no appropriate space for a headline you may want to place the headline outside the photo area. Indicate the color you want your headline to print in the margin or your layout. If you wish to print your headline in a color other than black or white, remember to include this color as a "special color" on your order form.

5. Indicate the position of additional copy with horizontal lines. It can be black or white, inside or outside the photo area. However, play it safe! Never indicate copy over patterned or mottled area of your photo, it will be difficult for your customers to read. Indicate the color you want your copy to print in the margin or your layout (figure D). Enclose a neatly typed version of your copy with your material.

6. You may use your company logo or other symbol on your printed job. Simply include a clean, camera-ready copy with your order, indicate it's size and location on your layout and indicate whether is should print in black or white. If you wish to print your logo in a color other than black or white, remember to include this color as a "special color" on your order form.

7. We can generate areas of special color to highlight type, dramatize photos or type. There is an additional charge for each special color. Draw a box on your layout where you wish the special color to appear and label it with a color letter, i.e. COLOR A. Include a swatch to indicate the color you desire and give it the same label letter (figure E). We will try to match your color as closely as possible with a "process screen tint" however, 100% perfect matches are rare.

8. Send all your material to us. We will analyze your project and call you if we need any additional instructions. Most print jobs take two to three weeks. If you require rush service please call us in advance for availability.

Remember, we are capable of many sizes and formats not listed in our price sheet. If you have special requirement, don't hesitate to call for a quotation.

PACIFIC

Event Professionals Profit from the New Print Technology

You've provided dazzling speakers, breath-taking entertainment delicious cuisine and a picturesque venue . . . but your documentation is deadly dull.

What will your client remember when he goes to his file to make next year's meeting decisions? Hopefully the reverie of your successes will linger long enough to make him/her dial your number again. The tangible element from any conference that can be filed and retained is the handbook, program or summery documentation. If its a boring one or two color stack of paper, stapled at the corner your chances of provoking fond memories are slim. Fortunately, the new electronic technology that is revolutionizing the printing industry is available to most event professionals. It can make both your point-of-event graphics and take-aways sing your praises with vivid color. Unfortunately, its also available to your competition. So, if you don't utilize it you can be sure they will.

The advances most applicable to the event professional fall into three categories:
1. Large scale presentation graphics,
2. LaserColor® graphics,
3. Data-to-press color printing.

Help Your Clients' Communicate
With Bold Color Banners, Charts & Murals

In the early 1980's large scale machines were developed to out-put the technical drawings of engineers and architects. These drawings, produced in computer programs called CAD (computer assisted design) became so complex that they required multi-color rendition. The generation of machines (or plotters) developed to cope with these drawings spawned a new graphics industry, *Plotter Graphics.* Today it is practical to produce full color posters, presentation boards, even billboards that include illustrations, photos, diagrams, charts and text. These plotter graphics require no printing plates and they can actually be run "one-off". This means you can customize your posters for every location in your venue. These paper wonders rival the color saturation of expensive photo murals. But unlike photo murals, they are easy to compose. Charts and graphs can be created and altered with a keystroke, then out-put minutes before a critical meeting. Thus, your client's data is always fresh.

A30

Plotter graphic systems are produced by a variety of manufacturers including Colossal Graphics (Palo Alto, CA), LaserMaster (Eden Prairie, MN) and ENCAD (San Diego, CA) and sold to service bureaus who make the out-put available to local graphic designers and ad agencies. For best results, the event planner should access plotter graphics through a design professional. After all, it makes little sense to pay the $10.00 to $12.00 per square foot the out-put costs unless the result is slick, professional and clearly communicates your clients' message.

The down side of plotter graphics is the thinness of the out-put paper which must be mounted or laminated to enjoy a life of more than two or three days. Dry mounting is necessary because the color dyes are not waterproof. Front and back mylar lamination (without ridged mounting) produces a great banner which can be rolled for storage or transportation.

If a more durable product is required the event planner can specify Scotchprint® Full-Color Graphics. This technique has many of the same characteristics of plotter graphics, but it can be applied to a variety of substrates including fabric and self adhesive vinyl. Scotchprint® Full-Color Graphics are sold through licensed distributors of the 3M Company. Although they are more durable they are generally more expensive than plotter graphics.

Other new poster techniques available to the event community include:
> **1. Bubble jet copiers.** These truly amazing color copiers will enlarge reflective artwork such as color logos, program covers and photographs to 24" x 36" with very little deterioration in image quality. They are a great way to produce small quantities of color posters quickly.
> **2. Iris prints** are the solution when highly accurate color is required in a poster or lecture presentation. Although these prints are costly, they are unrivalled for their resolution and color saturation. The are available in sizes up to 30" x 40".

Aside from the obvious applications as posters and banners, these oversized graphic techniques represent important ways meeting planners can help their clients dramatically express key concepts and themes, thus directly adding value to the event package.

Your Proposals Can Shout With Color

About the most useful innovation of the "desktop" era is the Cannon LaserColor® Printer. This versatile machine can; scan color images to disk, copy color transparencies and reflective art and output computer generated (and assembled) files. This means is there is no longer an excuse for dull, lifeless proposals, or sponsorship solicitations. Proposals can include the client's theme or promotional art, complete with lavish color photos of the corporate event buyer and his/her staff (talk about impressing the prospect.) Full color sponsorship solicitations can illustrate the previous year's event and include the ads and press coverage from which other sponsors benefitted. Although more than twenty or thirty of these packages are rarely needed, the cost of composition and output is easily justified by a moderate sized event.

Few things sells more effectively than well designed color presentations when event producers compete for corporate sponsorship. Instead of a timid presskit proposal you can create an oversized (11" x 17") presentation book for your event on the Cannon LaserColor® Printer. By using a Wire-O® binding on the 11" edge your book will open to a massive 11" x 34" color spread (hard for any corporate funding director to ignore.) Again, if you're not a design pro you would be well advised to consult one. They will ensure you get your money's worth from this exciting technology.

Scoop the Competition With Color Documentation

Most corporate and institutional conferences publish a summery document describing the event and capsulizing the important speakers comments. This documentation is seldom inspired because of the time-frame in which it must be produced. Today, we are entering an entirely new era in color printing that promises virtually instant documentation. We have all seen how desktop publishing speeds the composition of complex documents. Now, new printing press take the desktop data directly from disk to impression, by-passing the traditional film and plate bottle-necks of the past. The most widely accepted direct impression press is the Heidelberg GTO-DI. Its printing plates are mounted blank, with no image or type. Lasers generated by the presses own computer system interpret your file and etch the image in place, saving countless hours of tedious stripping and burning. The press then runs as a conventional four fountain unit.

The Heidelberg is a truly impressive advance, but nothing compared with the next generation press which is already on the market. The Indigo Digital Offset Color System is only slightly larger than a high-speed Xerox machine, yet it has the capacity to generate full color, ink-on-paper magazines at nearly conventional press speed. The trick lies in the total absence of printing plates as we know them. The image of each page is separately down-loaded from the system's powerful computer and held as an electrical charge on a printing cylinder just long enough to make a single impression. Each page is recycled four times (cyan, yellow, magenta, black) to create a full color image.

What Does It All Mean?

Most event planners have come to the profession through careers in catering or entertainment. They rarely understand the techniques or potential of graphic communication. Yet corporate and institutional meetings and events are, by their nature, exercises in communication. The event proposal that offers a rich, multi-layered communication matrix will be most likely to prevail. Expecting clients to accept mediocre graphics is like proposing a "lantern slide show" in the age of multimedia. A competent graphics professional can help you formulate dynamic proposals that capture broader, more profitable sales.

Richard Nodine is the recipient of over 20 national design awards for publications, corporate identity, collateral and packaging. He is a principal partner of Pacific Print Media, a San Francisco based sales promotion agency serving small to mid-sized companies, institutions and facilities.

A GUIDE TO THE CONCEPTS & TECHNIQUES OF SALES PROMOTION

PROFITABLE PROMOTIONS

GROW YOUR BUSINESS WITH THESE EASY PROMOTION CONCEPTS

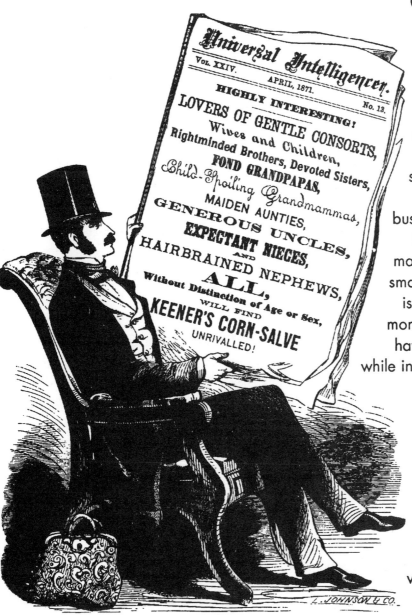

Today every business must promote just to survive. The Small Business Administration estimates that the average business looses 20 to 30% of it's customer base annually through attrition, competition or dissatisfaction, and one of the most common factors contributing to business failure is the lack of an effective sales promotion plan. Yet many businesses think they are too small to advertise. In this and future issues we will discuss some of the more creative options all businesses have to prospect for new business while increasing the profitability of their presant customers.

PLAN TO SUCCEED

The first step in developing a successful sales promotion campaign is to budget a specific percent of the annual gross revenues to sales promotion and development. The exact percent varies widely by type of business and size but there are established ranges for almost

> "Management's first responsibility is to answer the question; *what business are we in*".
>
> —Peter Drucker

every industry. Generally the percentage will decrease as the business grows and matures (becomes better known). You may find more useful guidelines for your business in trade publications.

As a general rule, sales promotion budgets range from 7% of a small businesses gross revenue to less than .05% for major corporations. However, these are guidelines and should not prevent the entrepreneur from radically departing from the norm. A highly successful national manufacturer of blue jeans once devoted a full 30% of their annual gross receipts to advertising. The important point is;   sales promotion must be properly integrated with your business plan, just like inventory or rent and occupancy costs. This requires accurately projecting both costs and <u>results</u>.

TELL THE WORLD WHAT YOU'RE DOING

Every business needs a "position paper". This is a statement of purpose. It is designed to tell the public what the business does, who it serves, and, most important, how your business is different from your competitions'. The position paper serves two important functions. Besides acting as a sales promotion vehicle, it also helps focus both staff and management's attention on the broad objectives of the organization. Peter Drucker said, "Management's first responsibility is to answer the question *what business are we in*". This is a function of the position paper.

Position papers may take many forms from a single typewritten sheet to a full color book. The most cost effective position papers achieve specific selling objectives while discussing general business goals. You might use a color brochure, showing your product line or discussing your services and telling your public what differentiates you from others in your field. Position papers are useful leave-behinds for salespersons. They more accurately describe your business than a simple calling card and (as with every other printed medium) they should be infused with added value, important information that will get them filed for future reference (more about this later).

Although a simple typewritten sheet is better than nothing, it should be your last resort. New businesses with limited public recognition are especially dependent on a good first impression. The well crafted position statement will do more per dollar to impress prospects and creditors than wood paneled offices and receptionists with exotic foreign accents.

A professionally designed logo should be an integral part of the position paper. A good logo communicates the essence of the organization and imparts the management's serious determination.

DEVELOP YOUR OWN HOT LIST OF PROSPECTS

Use low cost advertising to develop your own direct mail "hot list". Today the cost of postage has made the old "blanket mailing" approach to direct mail unrealistically expensive. If you aren't prepared to spend several thousand dollars on a clean, well structured mailing list your best bet is to use economical, small space classified and display ads to solicit prospect's names. If you sell to the general public, you may run your ads in large general circulation daily papers. But, you'll get a better return on your dollars if you can use special interest publications like business journals, local sports publications or professional newsletters.

The best strategy is to offer something of value in exchange for the prospect's response (sound familiar?). This entices the prospect while allowing you to establish a psychological obligation by supplying that value at no cost. Remember, small space ads seldom sell by themselves, they are merely a means of developing a prospective customer list.

BECOME AN EXPERT

Most business leaders have valuable trade or product knowledge their customers need. As long as there is no strategic disadvantage in sharing this information the business person can enrich his customer/client relationship by offering this information at little or no cost. A secondary benefit of free information is the greater ease with which well informed customers can be served. Well presented useful information is usually retained longer by the customer than mere ads or coupons. Frequently it can be filed for future reference, along with the businesses name and promotional material. Inexpensive information packages can be the most cost effective long-terms ads you can produce.

> To ensure retention of newsletters, enclude one or two pieces of information your client will consider vitally important.

Think of all the ways you could fill an 8 1/2" x 11" (or smaller) sheet of paper with important information your customers/clients want:

1. Recipes from a housewares retailer.

2. How to buy a mattress from a home furnishings store. Make a grid type chart of with your major styles listed down one side and the major benefits across the top. Place an x where styles and benefits coincide. This works well for any product that is generally sold in large assortments; stereos, personal stereos, tennis rackets, running shoes, etc.

3. Apply strategy #2 to the selection of a professional. No one says you have to be unbiased. After all, you are the best on your block. Dentists, chiropractors, bankers, insurance agents, consultants can all prepare a grid chart that shows why they are the best qualified to service most people's needs. Admitting that someone else might be more useful to a small segment of the population helps build credibility and is probably more honest.

4. Create a set of flash cards that make a modular pocket reference library. This technique is particularly useful for travel agents who book custom tours. You can provide your clients with a customized packet of 5" x 7" cards listing spots of interest in just those areas they will be visiting. They will appreciate not having to lug heavy guide books around and remember you the next time they travel.

   Other card ideas might include illustrated stretching exercises you can do in traffic or at your desk (Chiropractor), diagrams of basic knitting stitches (crafts shop), local high school or college teams' game schedule (sporting goods store).

BECOME A PUBLISHER

Consider publishing a series of reports, like a newsletter. A little extra time spent on the first one will pay off handsomely in future editions. Develop one appealing format and reuse it over a period of time. This is one of the efficiencies made possible by our modern computers with their vast storage capabilities. If the initial format is well conceived, future editions will require little design effort, thus saving time and money. The key to publishing an effective newsletter is the inclusion of one or two pieces of information your audience will consider vitally important. This will establish a retention value and encourage readers to keep your letters on file. Some business even give or sell customized binders to their customers to further encourage retention of letters.

Newsletters are especially effective for consultants and service businesses such as attorneys, accountants and commercial brokerage firms, people accustom to selling information. Although many professionals are initially concerned that they may be giving away their stock-in-trade, a well written newsletter will illustrate many new opportunities for their existing clients to access the firm's expertise. Furthermore, it will be difficult for your customers to take your competition seriously when you establish your business as the authority in your field. Soon your clients will have a massive reference volume generously endowed with your promotional messages.

Newsletters can also be useful to speciality merchants who sell high info-value wares and rely on repeat business. Examples include computer and/or software dealers, upscale camera stores or gourmet food shops. All have a constant flow of new products to offer and all have the ability to update their customers on new techniques and procedures.

GETTING THE MOST FOR YOUR COMMUNICATION DOLLAR

Current technology has placed typesetting and printing within the reach of virtually every business. Perhaps because of this, we are all barraged with thousands of messages daily. Unfortunately, most of those messages are simply blotted from our consciousness because they lack the basic "appeal" for which we screen all incoming data. The successful communicator knows some important tricks-of-the-trade to develop "appeal" and he uses them consistently.

WRITE FOR YOUR AUDIENCE

Plan your ads or presentations from your reader's point of view. This seems easy enough, but we see an amazing volume of material produced that has no interest to anyone but the writer. Ask yourself, "Why would anyone else want my information?" So many people write from an "I/me/we" point of view. The professional communicator writes from a "you" focus. For instance:

"Our staff of professional technicians will come to your home and clean your carpet and drapes with our state-of-the-art equipment."

"Your friends and family will admire the new-found luster and beauty of your carpet and draperies after a through cleaning by our professionals."

These two statements both promote the same offer but the first one focuses on the promoter. It tells the audience that their staff is professional and that they have state-of-the-art equipment. These are important "features" but features are secondary in the communication hierarchy. The professional communicator begins by telling his audience why they should listen to him, i.e. he lists the "benefits." *Benefits* are the things your *features* will do for your reader. Whenever you want someone to do something you must offer them benefits not features! You might have the most spectacular carpets and draperies in town but they would provide little satisfaction if no one noticed them. The cleaner in the first statement is offering dirt removal. The cleaner in the second statement is offering personal fulfillment. Which do think will sell more cleaning contracts?

TO WHOM ARE YOU SPEAKING?

Target advertising carefully. The most fascinating ad for steam turbines will be of relatively little interest to the average corporate secretary. To make sure your message is received and read by people who are truly interested use a competent list broker and independent media analyst.

Too often small advertisers try to economize by using cut-rate mailing lists and taking the advice of media sales people. There is no such thing as a cheep mailing list. The more refined your list, the more precisely you can target exactly those people who have an interest in your message. With today's postal rates, an un-refined list can be very expensive. The inexperienced advertiser who ventures into the mire of print and broadcast media buying will frequently fall prey to the self-proclaimed "media expert". These are usually nothing more than commissioned salesmen (usually with a background in used cars) who are armed with reams of data that seems to prove everything from the existence of life on Mars to the existence of chickens in Petaluma. Conversely, an independent media analyst (with no employer-driven bias) knows the successful delivery of your message at the lowest cost-per-thousand is the only thing that will insure repeat business. Good media buyers can be worth many times their small fee.

Good media buyers can be worth many times their small fee.

If you are still determined to place your own ads sans professional aid, at least use the old reliable acid test; "Are similar businesses consistently running similar ads in this media?" Even a fool won't use a given media when it doesn't deliver results. Ask your sales rep to show you a history of repeat ads placed by your close competition. This is the only way you can be sure you aren't single-handedly bearing the cost of exploring uncharted media waters.

CREATE APPROPRIATE IMAGERY

Create an information package appropriate to your message. If your primary message is "low-cost", heavy black type on rough yellow newsprint might be ideal. However, if your business is built on "discreet personal service" or "Old World Craftsmanship" you might want to consider another tact. A professional designer can advise you on the use of paper-stock, illustration, photography, type, foil stamping and special effects that will make your message more appealing to your prospects and readers. Frequently, these designers can save the business communicator thousands of dollars by helping them access stock illustration and photography, or by formatting information more efficiently.

TAP THE POWER OF LOW-COST COLOR

Color sells and today full color printing is within the budget of even the smallest businesses. If your business depends on the visual appeal of a product there is no more compelling sales tool than a well lighted photo . You may not have the budget to produce a full catalog, but most businesses can benefit from the use of color catalog sheets and postcards.

Everyone recognizes a postcards. They usually fall into one of two categories; the attractive, glossy, full color cards you get from friends

Most businesses can afford and benefit from the use of beautiful color catalog sheets and postcards.

on vacation and the less attractive one or two color cards that are used as sale notices by local merchants. Why not combine the two types of card for a surprisingly effective visual sales tool? If you or your suppliers have access to attractive product photos you can create colorful glossy postcards with off-price promotional copy on the back of the card.

We find this combination works best when you ask your customer to bring the card in to receive the special price or percentage off. In this way you can track the effectiveness of your promotion and create a "hot list" of name who have responded to direct-mail offers.

Glossy, full color cards are less apt to be treated like junk-mail. Many merchants even "hand write" (then print) their sales message, and others have their sales staff hand address the cards during slow periods. This extra personalization pays off in higher response. Prospects give a hand address card with a written message far greater attention than a conventional black red and white card with an address label.

A business with a more complex sales messages will find the catalog sheet the ideal partner to their sales letter. The conventional sales letter is probably still the mainstay of direct mail solicitation. Today, many businesses are equipped to generate merge-mail letters which achieve far higher rates of response. But the strongest opening presentation for most companies is the personalized letter with a page of color illustration.

Color photos help prospects visualize products and services and lend an air of authenticity to the small advertisers' presentation. Even service providers with no product to illustrate find that a color catalog sheet lends credibility to their promotions. Photos of the management and staff make an abstract service concept more human and believable. These catalog sheets are usually far less expensive than your customer's think they are, thus giving you an impressively big-look on a small budget.

The biggest cost in the production of full color material is usually the photo itself. Amateur photography is seldom satisfactory for product shots although good quality "candid" photography can be useful in selling services. Professional product shots can cost $300 and up. Still the dramatic impression made by well prepared color product sheets and postcards is usually well worth the investment.

Plan your cards and catalog sheets to serve multiple purposes. A trade show hand-out can also become a direct mail piece when teamed with a strong sales letter. Color postcards can be very flexible. One image can be printed in large quantities for economy, then customized on the back side with various messages throughout the year.

ADVANCE PLANNING MEANS BIG SAVINGS

Organize all your data before you begin. Know every point you want to make and list them in the order of their priority. This too seems incredibly basic but you would be surprised how many people want to edit their copy or include some previously forgotten point at the last minute. Excessive editing, even in computerized composition, wastes time, which of course, must equate to dollars.

Provide your copy writer with a list of major points you want to address. It's always helpful if you can describe your typical reader or show

> A long paper in which every item receives equal emphasis is boring and difficult to read.

the writer other papers that have been prepared for the same audience. If you write your own copy make it concise and, above all, legible. Its not difficult to understand that copy is frequently incorrect when it is keystroked from pages of scrawling penmanship that have been Xeroxed twice, then faxed. Naturally a good printer will correct their mistakes (even we make a few) at no cost to their clients. However, mistakes on pages keyed from illegible copy are considered ACs, (authors corrections) and they are billed at the printer's prevailing rates. Similarly, additions or revisions made after the initial input are considered ACs and the time required to key them is added to the client's invoice. This is costly enough when a project is still in "first draft", but it can be especially wasteful if done after a document has been formatted. Make changes in the early stages of a project. If you need the approval of others in your organization it is a good idea to get it on both the first draft and the final formatted version.

Use a fine red marker (Pilot Fineliner is good for this purpose) or pencil when making corrections to text or proofs. Place a carrot or arrow in the left margin of each line containing a correction, then indicate the correction as clearly as possible. If you fax the corrections the recipient will loose the benefit of the red marks. This can be acceptable if your notations are very neatly indicated. Keep a copy of your marked-up pages to assure all corrections were properly executed. This way you won't need to reread the entire document.

Prioritize your important points. A long paper in which every item receives equal emphasis is boring and difficult to read. Break your copy with internal headlines and "pull quotes" (larger type that repeats important concepts from the body of your text). In this way you will lead your reader through the text, allowing them to glean the major concepts easily.

Use "side boxes" (panels of type set off from the main text by a background color or rule lines) to explain concepts related to, but not essentially a part of your main text.

To avoid the cost of re-printing always print just a little more than you expect to need. Printing is cheep. Getting ready to print is expensive. After your job is on the press the incremental cost of each impression gets lower and lower as the press runs. However, once the press stops that incremental cost jumps back to the first impression cost.

Pacific Print Media is a full service agency offering communication service from concept to printing and mail management. We have over 30 years experience in corporate communications. Our goal is your total satisfaction with any printed material we produce. In-house computers and high quality Xerox machines make very rapid production possible. Furthermore, our vast experience in placing jobs with just the right printer assures our clients of the finest quality and very competitive prices. Let us show you how commanding your message can be when properly presented.

In future issues of our Profitable Promotions newsletter we will address topics like:
- how to increase profits with unique occasion and lifestyle packaging,
- how to maximize your trade show efforts,
- how to produce direct mail ads your customers will save of years,
- how to make your business cards work harder for you
- how to produce dramatic color brochures for under $100.00
- how to mail thousands of ads for as little as 2¢ each.

If you would like to receive future copies of this informative, and occasionally entertaining newsletter, please clip and return the postcard below. Please note any corrections on your mailing label, located on the reverse side. Thanks for your interest in Profitable Promotions!

PLEASE PLACE
FIRST CLASS
POSTAGE
HERE

PACIFIC PRINT MEDIA
251 POST STREET, SUITE 300
SAN FRANCISCO, CA 94108

PROFITABLE PROMOTIONS

- Does your businesses need to promote?

- How much should you spend on promotion?

- How can you get the maximum benefit for your promotion dollar?

- How can you afford the power of color in your low budget promotions?

- How can you mount promotions that make you look like a major player in your industry?

- This information and more is contained in your free introductory copy of Profitable Promotions!

- -

I find your perspectives on sales promotions valuable. Please continue to send me future editions of Profitable Promotions.

I am responsible for:

my company's sales promotion ☐

print buying ☐

neither ☐

I am planning: ☐

a direct mail campaign ☐

catalog ☐

annual report ☐

brochure ☐

postcard ☐

sell sheet ☐

newsletter ☐

menu ☐

poster ☐

Please contact me to arrange a free consultation. My phone number is :

( ) _____

ML